# ALA Survey of Librarian Salaries, 1984

Mary Jo Lynch, Project Director
Margaret Myers
Jeniece Guy

Office for Research and Office for Library Personnel Resources

American Library Association, 1984

Acknowledgements

The authors wish to thank the many respondents who filled in and returned the questionnaire. We are also grateful to Dan Wallace and the staff of the Library Research Center of the School of Library and Information Science at the University of Illinois for their careful and perceptive processing of this information. Finally, thanks are due Ruth Ann Jones, Sandra Raeside, and Pamela Arrington for careful typing of this report.

Library of Congress Catalog Card Number

ISBN 0-8389-3301-7
ISSN 0747-7201

Copyright © 1984 by the American Library Association. All rights reserved except those which may be granted by Sections 107 and 108 of the Copyright Revision Act of 1976.
Printed in the United States of America.

TABLE OF CONTENTS

INTRODUCTION

RESULTS

    Respondents   3

    Salaries
        Director   8
        Deputy/Associate Director   12
        Assistant Director   16
        Department Head/Branch Head   20
        Reference/Information Librarian   24
        Cataloger and/or Classifier   28
        Serials Librarian   32
        Audiovisual Librarian   36
        Government Documents Librarian   40
        Subject Specialist/Bibliographer   44
        Children's and/or Young Adult Services Librarian   48
        Adult Services Librarian   50
        Coordinator of Adult and/or Young Adult and/or Children's Services   52

    Employee Benefits   55

    Beginning Professionals   55

DISCUSSION

    Comments on Results   61
        Salaries by Position   61
        Salaries by Type of Library   61
        Salaries by Region of the U.S.   62
        Age Level Positions in Public Libraries   63

    Complicating Factors
        Meaning of "Full-Time"   65
        Meaning of "Professional"   66
        Salaries Below $8,000   66
        Job Levels or Status   66
        Employee Benefits   67

APPENDICES

    A.  Compensation and Employee Benefits
        1.  Employee Benefits: Basic Concepts and Current Issues   71
        2.  Salary Surveys Providing Information on Library Workers   78
        3.  ALA Policies Relating to Salary Issues   86
        4.  Selected Bibliography on Compensation and Employee Benefits   90
    B.  Technical Considerations   91
    C.  Cover Letter   95
    D.  Survey Questionnaire   97
    E.  Salaries Paid for Less than a 12 Month Year in Academic Libraries   105

## LIST OF TABLES

1. Small Public Libraries: Size of Group, Sample, Return   3
2. Large Public Libraries: Size of Group, Sample, Return   3
3. 2-year College Libraries: Size of Group, Sample, Return   4
4. 4-year College Libraries: Size of Group, Sample, Return   4
5. University Libraries: Size of Group, Sample, Return   4
6. All Libraries Surveyed: Size of Group, Sample, Return   5

Note: Tables 7A-21 present findings "by Type of Library and Region of the U.S." That phrase has been omitted from titles in the list below.

- 7A   Scheduled Salaries for Director   8
- 7B   Salaries Paid to Director   10
- 8A   Scheduled Salaries for Deputy/Associate Director   12
- 8B   Salaries Paid to Deputy/Associate Director   14
- 9A   Scheduled Salaries for Assistant Director   16
- 9B   Salaries Paid to Assistant Director   18
- 10A  Scheduled Salaries for Department Head/Branch Head   20
- 10B  Salaries Paid to Department Head/Branch Head   22
- 11A  Scheduled Salaries for Reference/Information Librarian   24
- 11B  Salaries Paid to Reference/Information Librarian   26
- 12A  Scheduled Salaries for Cataloger and/or Classifier   28
- 12B  Salaries Paid to Cataloger and/or Classifier   30
- 13A  Scheduled Salaries for Serials Librarian   32
- 13B  Salaries Paid to Serials Librarian   34
- 14A  Scheduled Salaries for Audiovisual Librarian   36
- 14B  Salaries Paid to Audiovisual Librarian   38
- 15A  Scheduled Salaries for Government Documents Librarian   40
- 15B  Salaries Paid to Government Documents Librarian   42
- 16A  Scheduled Salaries for Subject Specialist/Bibliographer   44
- 16B  Salaries Paid to Subject Specialist/Bibliographer   46
- 17A  Scheduled Salaries for Children's and/or Young Adult Services Librarian   48
- 17B  Salaries Paid to Children's and/or Young Adult Services Librarian   49
- 18A  Scheduled Salaries for Adult Services Librarian   50
- 18B  Salaries Paid to Adult Services Librarian   51
- 19A  Scheduled Salaries for Coordinator of Adult and/or Young Adult and/or Children's Services   52
- 19B  Salaries Paid to Coordinator of Adult and/or Young Adult and/or Children's Services   53
- 20   Employee Benefits as a Percentage of Total Payroll   56
- 21   Salaries Paid to Beginning Professionals   58
- 22   Rank Order of Position Titles by Mean of Scheduled Starting Salaries   64
- 23   Rank Order of Position Titles by Mean of Scheduled Maximum Salaries   64
- 24   Rank Order of Position Titles by Mean of Salaries Paid   65
- 25   States in Four Regions of the U.S.   93
- 26   Salaries Paid for Less than a 12 Month Year in Academic Libraries by Position and Type of Library   105

# 1

## INTRODUCTION

Librarians, the people who hire them, and interested others often ask the ALA Office for Library Personnel Resources (OLPR) to tell them what salary might be paid to a librarian in a particular position, working in a particular type of library, in a particular part of the U. S. This information is easily available for some positions, in some types of libraries and in some parts of the U.S., but there are significant gaps in the information which make it difficult to know what to expect for other positions, in other types of libraries and in other parts of the U.S.

To fill the need for information of this kind, the ALA Office for Library Personnel Resources began considering the idea of a periodic survey of salaries established for and paid to incumbents of particular positions. The ALA Office for Research (OFR) was consulted about this and agreed to direct such a survey in 1982. The results provided much of the needed information and the report was well received by the library community. The survey was repeated in 1984 with a few changes which will be described below.

Initially, OFR and OLPR thought that the universe for any ALA salary survey should include all types of libraries but we soon discovered that other sources cover the types of libraries not surveyed here. These sources are described in Appendix A-2. The ALA survey covers positions in two kinds of libraries: public libraries serving populations of at least 25,000 and academic libraries of all types.

The 1982 survey universe excluded members of the Association of Research Libraries (ARL) because information about salaries in those libraries is collected annually by ARL. That exclusion was not made in 1984. Since salaries in ARL libraries are generally higher than salaries in other libraries, the exclusion may have led readers of the report to conclude that library salaries in general are lower than they really are. Although the exclusion of ARL libraries was noted in the Introduction to the 1982 report, the note was not repeated in all places where the exclusion might have caused a lowering of the mean. To correct this distortion, ARL libraries were not excluded from the sample in 1984.

This report describes annual salaries scheduled for and paid to full-time professional positions. "Full-time" is not defined in the questionnaire, but instructions are given regarding split assignments and less than twelve month years. For the 1984 survey a change was made in those instructions. In 1982, respondents were asked to circle salaries that were for less than a twelve month year and an appendix to the 1982 report summarized how often this occurred for various positions in academic libraries. Reported salaries were recorded as given, however, and less than twelve month salaries were used in computing means. The 1984 questionnaire asked the respondent to circle the appropriate number of months if the salary was for less than a full year. A computer program was written to prorate these amounts to their twelve month equivalents and the twelve month figures were used in calculating means.

The survey asked for salaries paid to professional librarians. "Professional" was not defined, but each position was described on the questionnaire in such a way that professional responsibility was clearly implied. When people called to ask what was meant, we referred them to the ALA statement on "Library Education and Personnel Utilization."

The positions covered are those about which OLPR frequently gets requests for information. These positions are usually filled by persons trained to be librarians. Positions involving specialties for which training is customarily obtained outside the library field (e.g. personnel, data processing) were not included since salary surveys in the special fields involved are the best source of information about salaries for those positions (see Appendix A-2).

The positions covered in 1984 are the same as those covered in 1982 with one exception. In 1982 we asked about salaries for Children's and/or Young Adult and/or Adult Services Librarians and for two coordinator positions: Coordinator for Children's Services and Coordinator of Adult and/or Young Adult Services. In 1984 we asked about Children's and/or Young Adult Services Librarian and about Adult Services Librarian. The Coordinator positions for all age groups were combined.

One other change from 1982 should be noted. Nothing was said about contributed salaries on the 1982 questionnaire but returns sometimes noted that salaries were, at least partially, contributed and conversations with knowledgeable persons convinced us that including such figures was distorting our results. In 1984 the following instruction appeared on the questionnaire: "If services are contributed (i.e., institution pays some expenses or an honorarium but not a true salary) please do not list the incumbent."

In 1984 as in 1982, the questionnaire was directed to the employing institution rather than to individual employees, following a policy recommended by experts in the field of compensation.

The Library Research Center of the University of Illinois School of Library and Information Science performed the mailing, processing and analysis of the questionnaires using the Statistical Package for the Social Sciences (SPSS). ALA's OFR and OLPR used that analysis to produce this report.

Mary Jo Lynch, Director of ALA's Office for Research, directed the project and wrote this report with considerable assistance from Margaret Myers, Director of ALA's Office for Library Personnel Resources, and Jeniece Guy, Assistant Director of OLPR. OLPR had primary responsibility for Appendix A.

We hope the results of the survey will be useful to employers of librarians who need this information in administering an equitable pay plan and to librarians seeking employment or career advancement.

# 2
## RESULTS

Respondents

The survey questionnaire was mailed to 1418 randomly selected libraries in early January, 1984. Samples were drawn from twenty groups of libraries formed by stratifying five type-of-library categories by four regions of the U.S. Appendix B describes how groups were formed and sampled.

By the second week in March, useable responses had been received from 920 libraries, almost sixty-five percent of those selected. In addition, fourteen responses were unuseable for various reasons, nineteen were received too late for processing, and seventy-eight persons sent refusals. Tables 1-6 present statistics summarizing the initial mailing and rate of return for each group of libraries surveyed.

Table 1. Small Public Libraries: Size of Group, Sample, Return

|  | Group # | Sample # | % of group | Return # | % of sample |
|---|---|---|---|---|---|
| North Atlantic | 358 | 107 | 30 | 72 | 67 |
| Great Lakes and Plains | 320 | 96 | 30 | 68 | 71 |
| Southeast | 349 | 104 | 30 | 75 | 72 |
| West and Southwest | 230 | 69 | 30 | 50 | 82 |
| TOTAL | 1257 | 376 | 30 | 265 | 70 |

Table 2. Large Public Libraries: Size of Group, Sample, Return

|  | Group # | Sample # | % of group | Return # | % of sample |
|---|---|---|---|---|---|
| North Atlantic | 61 | 40 | 66 | 25 | 63 |
| Great Lakes and Plains | 83 | 49 | 59 | 48 | 98 |
| Southeast | 133 | 79 | 59 | 60 | 76 |
| West and Southwest | 119 | 71 | 60 | 54 | 76 |
| TOTAL | 396 | 239 | 60 | 187 | 78 |

Table 3. 2-Year College Libraries: Size of Group, Sample, Return

|  | Group # | Sample # | % of group | Return # | % of sample |
|---|---|---|---|---|---|
| North Atlantic | 296 | 65 | 22 | 22 | 34 |
| Southeast | 331 | 72 | 22 | 51 | 65 |
| Great Lakes and Plains | 338 | 74 | 22 | 49 | 69 |
| West and Southwest | 338 | 74 | 22 | 169 | 59 |
| TOTAL | 1303 | 285 | 22 | 169 | 59 |

Table 4. 4-Year College Libraries: Size of Group, Sample, Return

|  | Group # | Sample # | % of group | Return # | % of sample |
|---|---|---|---|---|---|
| North Atlantic | 187 | 61 | 33 | 28 | 46 |
| Southeast | 244 | 80 | 33 | 48 | 60 |
| Great Lakes and Plains | 193 | 63 | 33 | 30 | 48 |
| West and Southwest | 115 | 40 | 35 | 17 | 43 |
| TOTAL | 739 | 244 | 33 | 123 | 50 |

Table 5. University Libraries: Size of Group, Sample, Return

|  | Group # | Sample # | % of group | Return # | % of sample |
|---|---|---|---|---|---|
| North Atlantic | 419 | 92 | 22 | 42 | 46 |
| Southeast | 305 | 67 | 22 | 41 | 61 |
| Great Lakes and Plains | 221 | 49 | 22 | 38 | 78 |
| West and Southwest | 302 | 66 | 22 | 55 | 83 |
| TOTAL | 1247 | 274 | 22 | 176 | 54 |

Table 6. All Libraries Surveyed: Size of Group, Sample, Return

|  | Group # | Sample # | % of group | Return # | % of sample |
|---|---|---|---|---|---|
| North Atlantic | 1321 | 365 | 28 | 189 | 52 |
| Southeast | 1283 | 364 | 28 | 252 | 69 |
| Great Lakes and Plains | 1234 | 369 | 30 | 254 | 69 |
| West and Southwest | 1104 | 320 | 29 | 225 | 70 |
| TOTAL | 4942 | 1418 | 29 | 920 | 65 |

Although Tables 1 through 6 are useful in presenting a description of survey respondents as a whole, it is important to note that the number of respondents providing information which contributed to the tables in this chapter varies widely from position to position and by type of information involved. The number of responses reporting salaries for a particular position, in a particular type of library, in a particular part of the U.S., is often too small to permit generalizations (i.e., less than twenty-five cases). However, the number of respondents is often considerably more than twenty-five when only two variables are considered (i.e., position and type of library or position and area of the country.) The work involved in achieving a similar level of response for all position/library type/geographical area cells in the tables would probably drive the costs of conducting the survey to levels unacceptable in the library community.

## Salaries

The questionnaire asked for two different kinds of information about each position. First the respondent was asked to indicate:

ANNUAL SALARY RANGE: (from your formal salary schedule)

Starting_____

Maximum_____

Then the respondent was asked to list the annual salary of each incumbent.

In this report two different kinds of findings are presented. First the salary ranges for each position are summarized in a "Scheduled Salaries" table (Table A). Then the annual salary paid to incumbents of the position are summarized in a "Salaries Paid" table (Table B).

Different libraries provided information on different positions. Responses also varied in other ways. Some libraries provided information on scheduled salaries but not on salaries paid to incumbents. There are probably several reasons for this response but two were explained to us by respondents: the number of incumbents was so large that the respondent could not provide specific data; or local regulations prohibit release of specific salaries.

Some libraries provided information on starting salaries for several positions but did not provide information on maximum salaries. A few did the reverse. Some libraries provided information on salaries paid to incumbents of various positions but did not give scheduled salaries. When this was explained to us, respondents noted either that no range existed or that ranges were currently under negotiation.

Because of this variety, the number of cases involved (N) is indicated for each individual mean presented on the tables. The reader should be aware that means resulting from a very small number of cases are much less representative of all libraries in a particular group than means resulting from a larger number of cases.

The tables which follow (Tables 7A & 7B through 19A & 19B) are arranged by position title. For each of thirteen positions, Table A presents scheduled salaries and Table B presents salaries paid to incumbents. For each position and each group of libraries, the Scheduled Salary table records the lowest, the highest, and the mean of all reported starting salaries and the lowest, highest, and mean of all maximum salaries reported. In parentheses below each mean is a note of how many libraries contributed to the figure.

The Salaries Paid table records, for each group of libraries, the lowest salary, the highest salary, and the mean salary. On Table B the number in parentheses below the mean salary figure is the number of incumbents whose salary is reported, not the number of libraries.

Tables 7 A&B through 16 A&B report on positions found in all five types of libraries. Tables 17 A&B through 19 A&B report on positions found mainly in public libraries and rows for the three kinds of academic libraries have been removed from the table shell.

Respondents were asked to report salaries as of January, 1984.

Table 7A. Scheduled Salaries for Director by Type of Library and Region of the U.S. (in dollars)

| Region | North Atlantic | | | | | | Great Lakes and Plains | | | | | |
|---|---|---|---|---|---|---|---|---|---|---|---|---|
| | Starting | | | Maximum | | | Starting | | | Maximum | | |
| Type of Library | Low | Mean | High | Low | Mean | High | Low | Mean | High | Low | Mean | High |
| Small Public* | 9,000 | 23,398 N=31 | 32,510 | 15,000 | 30,397 N=28 | 50,253 | 12,000 | 24,550 N=29 | 36,215 | 22,489 | 34,485 N=21 | 45,000 |
| Large Public** | 19,000 | 28,706 N=12 | 40,441 | 25,000 | 39,254 N=11 | 54,041 | 25,000 | 36,706 N=15 | 59,888 | 30,000 | 45,975 N=13 | 74,496 |
| 2-year College | 13,000 | 23,413 N=16 | 37,000 | 20,000 | 32,310 N=12 | 44,000 | 9,500 | 21,539 N=31 | 39,540 | 12,500 | 35,972 N=31 | 54,321 |
| 4-year College | 15,499 | 24,585 N=14 | 35,160 | 20,133 | 37,459 N=10 | 50,144 | 12,800 | 18,764 N=6 | 23,820 | 22,667 | 27,521 N=3 | 34,896 |
| Univ. | 13,000 | 31,558 N=15 | 50,000 | 24,000 | 50,908 N=13 | 100,000 | 10,000 | 24,594 N=10 | 40,000 | 10,500 | 32,674 N=9 | 60,000 |
| All | 9,000 | 25,704 N=88 | 50,000 | 15,000 | 36,581 N=74 | 100,000 | 9,500 | 25,151 N=91 | 59,888 | 10,500 | 36,540 N=78 | 74,496 |

*Small public = public library serving a population of from 25,000 to 99,999.
**Large public = public library serving a population of over 100,000.

N = number of libraries

Source: ALA SURVEY OF LIBRARIAN SALARIES, 1984

Table 7A.(cont.) Scheduled Salaries for Director by Type of Library and Region of the U.S. (in dollars)

| Region | Southeast | | | | | | West and Southwest | | | | | | All Libraries | | | | | |
|---|---|---|---|---|---|---|---|---|---|---|---|---|---|---|---|---|---|---|
| | Starting | | | Maximum | | | Starting | | | Maximum | | | Starting | | | Maximum | | |
| Type of Library | Low | Mean | High | Low | Mean | High | Low | Mean | High | Low | Mean | High | Low | Mean | High | Low | Mean | High |
| Small Public* | 9,000 | 18,250 N=47 | 29,744 | 13,900 | 27,690 N=37 | 47,311 | 13,600 | 28,263 N=35 | 42,414 | 17,358 | 36,222 N=33 | 52,000 | 9,000 | 23,128 N=142 | 42,414 | 13,900 | 31,892 N=119 | 52,000 |
| Large Public** | 15,523 | 27,697 N=39 | 41,727 | 19,300 | 39,045 N=39 | 58,957 | 22,818 | 37,362 N=41 | 69,927 | 29,162 | 48,613 N=39 | 86,882 | 15,523 | 32,776 N=107 | 69,927 | 19,300 | 43,609 N=102 | 86,882 |
| 2-year College | 11,000 | 18,715 N=28 | 32,956 | 18,000 | 31,276 N=20 | 44,265 | 14,780 | 30,332 N=30 | 55,948 | 23,000 | 42,705 N=29 | 98,280 | 9,500 | 23,584 N=105 | 55,948 | 12,500 | 36,595 N=92 | 98,280 |
| 4-year College | 9,600 | 14,533 N=3 | 19,500 | 9,900 | 19,700 N=2 | 29,500 | 18,500 | 20,592 N=4 | 23,067 | 20,000 | 26,800 N=4 | 39,600 | 9,600 | 21,583 N=27 | 35,160 | 9,900 | 31,776 N=19 | 50,144 |
| Univ. | 15,000 | 23,637 N=6 | 29,124 | 18,000 | 36,166 N=5 | 49,812 | 13,200 | 31,725 N=16 | 47,700 | 13,200 | 47,188 N=14 | 71,449 | 10,000 | 29,122 N=47 | 50,000 | 10,500 | 43,837 N=41 | 100,000 |
| All | 9,000 | 21,523 N=123 | 41,727 | 9,900 | 32,942 N=103 | 58,957 | 13,200 | 31,912 N=126 | 69,927 | 13,200 | 42,836 N=119 | 98,280 | 9,000 | 26,213 N=428 | 69,927 | 9,900 | 37,563 N=373 | 100,000 |

*Small public = public library serving a population of from 25,000 to 99,999.
**Large public = public library serving a population of over 100,000.

N = number of libraries

Source: ALA SURVEY OF LIBRARIAN SALARIES, 1984

Table 7B. Salaries Paid to Director by Type of Library and Region of the U.S. (in dollars)

| Region<br>Type of Library | North Atlantic | | | Great Lakes and Plains | | |
|---|---|---|---|---|---|---|
| | Low | Mean | High | Low | Mean | High |
| Small Public* | 11,400 | 29,128<br>N=65 | 50,300 | 16,078 | 28,172<br>N=59 | 41,981 |
| Large Public** | 22,000 | 37,939<br>N=20 | 62,644 | 28,828 | 41,858<br>N=38 | 71,146 |
| 2-year College | 21,409 | 30,618<br>N=20 | 50,295 | 10,200 | 30,292<br>N=45 | 54,321 |
| 4-year College | 14,000 | 30,335<br>N=22 | 50,144 | 14,000 | 24,678<br>N=36 | 44,300 |
| Univ. | 14,600 | 38,453<br>N=37 | 92,000 | 10,500 | 36,558<br>N=34 | 70,000 |
| All | 11,400 | 32,650<br>N=164 | 92,000 | 10,200 | 31,827<br>N=212 | 71,146 |

*Small public = public library serving a population of from 25,000 to 99,999.
**Large public = public library serving a population of over 100,000.

N = number of incumbents

Source: ALA SURVEY OF LIBRARIAN SALARIES, 1984

Table 7B.(cont.)  Salaries Paid to Director
by Type of Library and Region of the U.S.
(in dollars)

| Region | Southeast | | | West and Southwest | | | All Libraries | | |
|---|---|---|---|---|---|---|---|---|---|
| Type of Library | Low | Mean | High | Low | Mean | High | Low | Mean | High |
| Small Public* | 8,000 | 20,942 N=71 | 39,874 | 15,750 | 32,307 N=46 | 52,000 | 8,000 | 27,090 N=241 | 52,000 |
| Large Public** | 16,800 | 34,900 N=55 | 58,957 | 29,162 | 44,569 N=50 | 77,945 | 16,800 | 39,861 N=163 | 77,945 |
| 2-year College | 13,466 | 25,837 N=43 | 44,265 | 20,000 | 35,099 N=42 | 66,996 | 10,200 | 30,404 N=150 | 66,996 |
| 4-year College | 9,900 | 23,598 N=29 | 36,000 | 17,900 | 22,564 N=13 | 29,400 | 9,900 | 25,335 N=100 | 50,144 |
| Univ. | 15,000 | 37,191 N=34 | 68,000 | 13,200 | 39,953 N=50 | 67,392 | 10,500 | 38,244 N=155 | 92,000 |
| All | 8,000 | 27,872 N=232 | 68,000 | 13,200 | 37,213 N=201 | 77,945 | 8,000 | 32,198 N=809 | 92,000 |

 *Small public = public library serving a population of from 25,000 to 99,999.
**Large public = public library serving a population of over 100,000.

N = number of incumbents

Source:  ALA SURVEY OF LIBRARIAN SALARIES, 1984

Table 8A. Scheduled Salaries for Deputy/Associate Director by Type of Library and Region of the U.S. (in dollars)

| Region | North Atlantic | | | | | | Great Lakes and Plains | | | | | |
|---|---|---|---|---|---|---|---|---|---|---|---|---|
| | Starting | | | Maximum | | | Starting | | | Maximum | | |
| Type of Library | Low | Mean | High | Low | Mean | High | Low | Mean | High | Low | Mean | High |
| Small Public* | 11,800 | 20,298 N=19 | 31,254 | 14,200 | 26,281 N=18 | 41,343 | 11,780 | 18,714 N=17 | 28,561 | 15,476 | 24,751 N=17 | 32,490 |
| Large Public** | 18,000 | 25,712 N=13 | 38,000 | 23,000 | 34,153 N=12 | 41,583 | 16,500 | 25,852 N=21 | 46,046 | 20,530 | 35,618 N=21 | 58,760 |
| 2-year College | 16,338 | 21,191 N=4 | 24,586 | 30,420 | 37,695 N=4 | 52,769 | 21,887 | 23,792 N=3 | 25,081 | 37,546 | 42,489 N=3 | 50,927 |
| 4-year College | 14,000 | 19,116 N=6 | 26,590 | 24,614 | 30,439 N=6 | 37,008 | 16,619 | 19,798 N=2 | 22,977 | 26,337 | 28,062 N=2 | 29,788 |
| Univ. | 13,000 | 26,081 N=13 | 35,000 | 30,066 | 40,209 N=10 | 51,629 | 20,580 | 25,829 N=6 | 30,000 | 30,144 | 36,736 N=5 | 44,898 |
| All | 11,800 | 22,881 N=55 | 38,000 | 14,200 | 32,368 N=50 | 52,769 | 11,780 | 23,000 N=49 | 46,046 | 15,476 | 32,001 N=48 | 58,760 |

*Small public = public library serving a population of from 25,000 to 99,999.
**Large public = public library serving a population of over 100,000.

N = number of libraries

Source: ALA SURVEY OF LIBRARIAN SALARIES, 1984

Table 8A.(cont.) Scheduled Salaries for Deputy/Associate Director by Type of Library and Region of the U.S. (in dollars)

| Region | Southeast | | | | | | West and Southwest | | | | | | All Libraries | | | | | |
|---|---|---|---|---|---|---|---|---|---|---|---|---|---|---|---|---|---|---|
| | Starting | | | Maximum | | | Starting | | | Maximum | | | Starting | | | Maximum | | |
| Type of Library | Low | Mean | High | Low | Mean | High | Low | Mean | High | Low | Mean | High | Low | Mean | High | Low | Mean | High |
| Small Public* | 9,000 | 15,114 N=17 | 20,473 | 12,168 | 23,197 N=13 | 30,727 | 10,152 | 23,487 N=16 | 38,064 | 13,584 | 29,377 N=16 | 46,580 | 9,000 | 19,370 N=69 | 38,064 | 12,168 | 26,022 N=64 | 46,580 |
| Large Public** | 9,394 | 22,098 N=30 | 34,059 | 13,484 | 31,210 N=29 | 50,321 | 16,058 | 28,860 N=38 | 51,678 | 19,512 | 37,258 N=37 | 64,206 | 13,484 | 25,851 N=102 | 51,678 | 13,484 | 34,762 N=99 | 64,206 |
| 2-year College | 12,500 | 17,161 N=8 | 22,944 | 13,527 | 24,403 N=5 | 39,562 | 14,000 | 21,460 N=6 | 32,603 | 15,875 | 33,586 N=6 | 49,696 | 13,527 | 20,104 N=21 | 32,603 | 13,527 | 33,432 N=18 | 52,769 |
| 4-year College | -- | -- N=0 | -- | -- | -- N=0 | -- | -- | 15,500 N=1 | -- | -- | 17,500 N=1 | -- | 14,000 | 18,866 N=9 | 26,590 | 17,500 | 28,473 N=9 | 37,008 |
| Univ. | -- | 22,140 N=1 | -- | -- | 36,900 N=1 | -- | 12,000 | 25,374 N=10 | 34,860 | 16,000 | 37,907 N=10 | 51,000 | 12,000 | 25,664 N=30 | 35,000 | 16,000 | 38,529 N=26 | 51,629 |
| All | 9,000 | 19,273 N=56 | 34,059 | 12,168 | 28,449 N=48 | 50,321 | 10,152 | 26,344 N=71 | 51,678 | 13,584 | 34,952 N=70 | 64,206 | 9,000 | 23,096 N=231 | 51,678 | 12,168 | 32,253 N=216 | 64,206 |

*Small public = public library serving a population of from 25,000 to 99,999.
**Large public = public library serving a population of over 100,000.

N = number of libraries

Source: ALA SURVEY OF LIBRARIAN SALARIES, 1984

Table 8B. Salaries Paid to Deputy/
Associate Director by Type of Library
and Region of the U.S. (in dollars)

| Region<br>Type of Library | North Atlantic | | | Great Lakes and Plains | | |
|---|---|---|---|---|---|---|
| | Low | Mean | High | Low | Mean | High |
| Small Public* | 8,699 | 23,683<br>N=27 | 40,620 | 12,600 | 22,122<br>N=31 | 33,000 |
| Large Public** | 20,280 | 34,076<br>N=20 | 45,438 | 19,011 | 31,904<br>N=33 | 64,033 |
| 2-year College | 18,011 | 30,018<br>N=7 | 45,735 | 18,043 | 30,475<br>N=6 | 50,927 |
| 4-year College | 10,500 | 23,315<br>N=13 | 31,830 | 14,000 | 18,672<br>N=6 | 28,400 |
| Univ. | 20,025 | 35,000<br>N=27 | 52,900 | 14,500 | 30,601<br>N=14 | 41,304 |
| All | 8,699 | 29,566<br>N=94 | 52,900 | 12,600 | 27,355<br>N=90 | 64,033 |

*Small public = public library serving a population of from 25,000 to 99,999.
**Large public = public library serving a population of over 100,000.

N = number of incumbents

Source: ALA SURVEY OF LIBRARIAN SALARIES, 1984

Table 8B.(cont.) Salaries Paid to Deputy/
Associate Director by Type of Library and
Region of the U.S. (in dollars)

| Region | Southeast | | | West and Southwest | | | All Libraries | | |
|---|---|---|---|---|---|---|---|---|---|
| Type of Library | Low | Mean | High | Low | Mean | High | Low | Mean | High |
| Small Public* | 9,000 | 17,097 N=25 | 24,601 | 13,584 | 25,679 N=15 | 38,603 | 8,699 | 21,815 N=98 | 40,620 |
| Large Public** | 12,762 | 28,508 N=32 | 43,469 | 16,058 | 33,354 N=51 | 64,206 | 12,762 | 31,968 N=136 | 64,206 |
| 2-year College | 15,456 | 21,055 N=10 | 39,562 | 12,500 | 24,612 N=8 | 41,283 | 12,500 | 25,820 N=31 | 50,927 |
| 4-year College | 15,000 | 16,940 N=5 | 18,400 | -- | 17,000 N=1 | -- | 10,500 | 20,673 N=25 | 31,830 |
| Univ. | 23,150 | 34,927 N=16 | 50,650 | 13,000 | 33,706 N=44 | 47,300 | 13,000 | 33,815 N=101 | 52,900 |
| All | 9,000 | 24,929 N=88 | 50,650 | 12,500 | 31,792 N=119 | 64,206 | 8,699 | 28,691 N=391 | 64,206 |

 *Small public = public library serving a population of from 25,000 to 99,999.
**Large public = public library serving a population of over 100,000.

N = number of incumbents

Source:  ALA SURVEY OF LIBRARIAN SALARIES, 1984

Table 9A. Scheduled Salaries for Assistant Director by Type of Library and Region of the U.S. (in dollars)

| Region | North Atlantic | | | | | | Great Lakes and Plains | | | | | |
|---|---|---|---|---|---|---|---|---|---|---|---|---|
| | Starting | | | Maximum | | | Starting | | | Maximum | | |
| Type of Library | Low | Mean | High | Low | Mean | High | Low | Mean | High | Low | Mean | High |
| Small Public* | 15,192 | 17,225 N=9 | 19,419 | 18,000 | 24,667 N=8 | 37,020 | 13,640 | 18,259 N=4 | 28,135 | 16,056 | 21,344 N=3 | 29,425 |
| Large Public** | 17,375 | 22,593 N=11 | 33,000 | 25,161 | 29,852 N=11 | 37,263 | 20,352 | 27,384 N=10 | 37,180 | 26,784 | 38,071 N=10 | 55,596 |
| 2-year College | 11,400 | 16,910 N=6 | 24,296 | 14,600 | 27,328 N=4 | 52,769 | 18,067 | 21,550 N=4 | 24,150 | 38,064 | 44,729 N=4 | 54,321 |
| 4-year College | 24,180 | 24,564 N=2 | 24,948 | 33,684 | 34,363 N=2 | 35,042 | 12,000 | 13,650 N=2 | 15,300 | -- | -- N=0 | -- |
| Univ. | 13,000 | 23,337 N=9 | 30,000 | 34,691 | 39,652 N=7 | 48,396 | 16,000 | 22,824 N=4 | 28,080 | 18,000 | 31,167 N=4 | 39,040 |
| All | 11,400 | 20,653 N=37 | 33,000 | 14,600 | 30,666 N=32 | 52,769 | 12,000 | 22,987 N=24 | 37,180 | 16,056 | 35,634 N=21 | 55,596 |

*Small public = public library serving a population of from 25,000 to 99,999.
**Large public = public library serving a population of over 100,000.

N = number of libraries

Source: ALA SURVEY OF LIBRARIAN SALARIES, 1984

Table 9A.(cont.) Scheduled Salaries for Assistant Director by Type of Library and Region of the U.S. (in dollars)

| Region | Southeast | | | | | | West and Southwest | | | | | | All Libraries | | | | | |
|---|---|---|---|---|---|---|---|---|---|---|---|---|---|---|---|---|---|---|
| | Starting | | | Maximum | | | Starting | | | Maximum | | | Starting | | | Maximum | | |
| Type of Library | Low | Mean | High | Low | Mean | High | Low | Mean | High | Low | Mean | High | Low | Mean | High | Low | Mean | High |
| Small Public* | 9,000 | 15,229 N=9 | 21,000 | 12,500 | 21,580 N=8 | 27,475 | 11,000 | 22,750 N=10 | 34,091 | 14,040 | 28,853 N=10 | 40,664 | 9,000 | 18,519 N=32 | 34,091 | 12,500 | 24,915 N=29 | 40,664 |
| Large Public** | 15,158 | 21,693 N=17 | 26,102 | 19,076 | 31,032 N=17 | 45,792 | 21,100 | 27,667 N=21 | 40,862 | 26,373 | 36,053 N=20 | 57,440 | 15,158 | 24,952 N=59 | 40,862 | 19,076 | 33,753 N=58 | 57,440 |
| 2-year College | 18,325 | 21,663 N=2 | 25,000 | 28,885 | 34,393 N=2 | 39,900 | 22,240 | 30,620 N=2 | 39,000 | 36,656 | 39,828 N=2 | 43,000 | 14,600 | 20,873 N=14 | 39,000 | 14,600 | 36,389 N=12 | 54,321 |
| 4-year College | -- | 13,000 N=1 | -- | -- | -- N=0 | -- | -- | 18,480 N=1 | -- | -- | 19,080 N=1 | -- | 12,000 | 17,985 N=6 | 24,948 | 19,080 | 29,269 N=3 | 35,042 |
| Univ. | 16,380 | 19,040 N=2 | 21,700 | -- | 22,724 N=1 | -- | 10,000 | 21,893 N=8 | 31,200 | 14,500 | 35,582 N=6 | 49,400 | 10,000 | 22,372 N=23 | 31,200 | 14,500 | 35,469 N=18 | 49,400 |
| All | 9,000 | 19,362 N=31 | 26,102 | 12,500 | 28,275 N=28 | 45,792 | 10,000 | 25,318 N=42 | 40,862 | 14,040 | 33,893 N=39 | 57,440 | 9,000 | 22,235 N=134 | 40,862 | 12,500 | 32,026 N=120 | 57,440 |

*Small public = public library serving a population of from 25,000 to 99,999.
**Large public = public library serving a population of over 100,000.

N = number of libraries

Source: ALA SURVEY OF LIBRARIAN SALARIES, 1984

Table 9B. Salaries Paid to Assistant Director by Type of Library and Region of the U.S. (in dollars)

| Region<br>Type of Library | North Atlantic | | | Great Lakes and Plains | | |
|---|---|---|---|---|---|---|
| | Low | Mean | High | Low | Mean | High |
| Small Public* | 9,700 | 21,377<br>N=10 | 26,137 | 11,700 | 19,209<br>N=9 | 29,425 |
| Large Public** | 17,404 | 30,760<br>N=24 | 37,263 | 22,008 | 36,204<br>N=27 | 55,596 |
| 2-year College | 12,700 | 26,399<br>N=6 | 40,640 | 16,701 | 33,332<br>N=6 | 50,927 |
| 4-year College | 14,800 | 22,259<br>N=3 | 27,030 | 12,000 | 18,710<br>N=9 | 26,250 |
| Univ. | 18,100 | 32,742<br>N=23 | 54,000 | 15,595 | 28,921<br>N=18 | 42,200 |
| All | 9,700 | 29,246<br>N=66 | 54,000 | 11,700 | 29,556<br>N=69 | 55,596 |

 *Small public = public library serving a population of from 25,000 to 99,999.
**Large public = public library serving a population of over 100,000.

N = number of incumbents

Source: ALA SURVEY OF LIBRARIAN SALARIES, 1984

Table 9B.(cont.) Salaries Paid to Assistant Director by Type of Library and Region of the U.S. (in dollars)

| Region<br>Type of Library | Southeast | | | West and Southwest | | | All Libraries | | |
|---|---|---|---|---|---|---|---|---|---|
| | Low | Mean | High | Low | Mean | High | Low | Mean | High |
| Small Public* | 8,000 | 16,883<br>N=14 | 24,420 | 13,411 | 28,305<br>N=18 | 37,829 | 8,000 | 22,206<br>N=51 | 37,829 |
| Large Public** | 15,863 | 27,876<br>N=36 | 35,879 | 20,544 | 32,800<br>N=40 | 50,759 | 15,863 | 31,742<br>N=127 | 55,596 |
| 2-year College | 16,651 | 23,792<br>N=7 | 38,836 | 20,000 | 22,283<br>N=3 | 25,253 | 12,700 | 26,514<br>N=24 | 50,927 |
| 4-year College | 16,956 | 22,175<br>N=3 | 26,042 | -- | --<br>N=0 | -- | 12,000 | 20,113<br>N=15 | 27,030 |
| Univ. | 17,000 | 31,324<br>N=18 | 50,194 | 12,000 | 31,335<br>N=45 | 43,920 | 12,000 | 31,227<br>N=104 | 54,000 |
| All | 8,000 | 26,113<br>N=78 | 50,194 | 12,000 | 30,954<br>N=108 | 50,759 | 8,000 | 29,126<br>N=321 | 55,596 |

 *Small public = public library serving a population of from 25,000 to 99,999.
 **Large public = public library serving a population of over 100,000.

N = number of incumbents

Source:  ALA SURVEY OF LIBRARIAN SALARIES, 1984

Table 10A. Scheduled Salaries for Department Head/Branch Head by Type of Library and Region of the U.S. (in dollars)

| Region | North Atlantic | | | | | | Great Lakes and Plains | | | | | |
|---|---|---|---|---|---|---|---|---|---|---|---|---|
| | Starting | | | Maximum | | | Starting | | | Maximum | | |
| Type of Library | Low | Mean | High | Low | Mean | High | Low | Mean | High | Low | Mean | High |
| Small Public* | 9,300 | 15,899 N=29 | 25,889 | 14,200 | 21,533 N=28 | 35,843 | 8,507 | 16,432 N=28 | 30,727 | 11,357 | 22,571 N=27 | 39,216 |
| Large Public** | 11,000 | 17,076 N=21 | 23,608 | 12,000 | 25,874 N=21 | 36,816 | 10,920 | 17,812 N=42 | 27,196 | 15,642 | 25,773 N=41 | 42,492 |
| 2-year College | 15,207 | 19,458 N=3 | 23,558 | 30,170 | 34,358 N=3 | 38,550 | 22,096 | 23,609 N=2 | 25,123 | 38,796 | 39,249 N=2 | 39,702 |
| 4-year College | 15,893 | 19,101 N=4 | 22,628 | 28,470 | 29,511 N=2 | 30,552 | -- | 10,667 N=1 | -- | -- | -- N=0 | -- |
| Univ. | 16,531 | 22,143 N=11 | 29,535 | 30,066 | 40,172 N=9 | 50,144 | 16,615 | 19,658 N=9 | 25,000 | 20,448 | 28,754 N=7 | 35,000 |
| All | 9,300 | 17,618 N=68 | 29,535 | 12,000 | 26,506 N=63 | 50,144 | 8,507 | 17,598 N=82 | 30,727 | 11,357 | 25,271 N=77 | 42,492 |

*Small public = public library serving a population of from 25,000 to 99,999.
**Large public = public library serving a population of over 100,000.

N = number of libraries

Source: ALA SURVEY OF LIBRARIAN SALARIES, 1984

Table 10A.(cont.) Scheduled Salaries for Department Head/Branch Head by Type of Library and Region of the U.S. (in dollars)

| Region | Southeast | | | | | | West and Southwest | | | | | | All Libraries | | | | | |
|---|---|---|---|---|---|---|---|---|---|---|---|---|---|---|---|---|---|---|
| | Starting | | | Maximum | | | Starting | | | Maximum | | | Starting | | | Maximum | | |
| Type of Library | Low | Mean | High | Low | Mean | High | Low | Mean | High | Low | Mean | High | Low | Mean | High | Low | Mean | High |
| Small Public* | 8,500 | 12,961 N=17 | 15,964 | 9,500 | 18,547 N=14 | 22,724 | 13,538 | 20,393 N=23 | 31,616 | 18,012 | 26,117 N=23 | 37,586 | 8,500 | 16,604 N=97 | 31,616 | 9,500 | 22,529 N=92 | 39,216 |
| Large Public** | 8,268 | 15,546 N=51 | 24,804 | 11,963 | 24,217 N=51 | 36,130 | 13,499 | 20,799 N=47 | 34,191 | 16,449 | 28,382 N=46 | 60,176 | 8,268 | 17,870 N=161 | 34,191 | 11,963 | 26,042 N=159 | 60,176 |
| 2-year College | 17,000 | 21,251 N=3 | 25,000 | 34,759 | 38,386 N=3 | 40,500 | 23,784 | 26,503 N=3 | 30,559 | 38,367 | 45,745 N=3 | 51,855 | 30,170 | 22,623 N=11 | 30,559 | 30,170 | 39,451 N=11 | 51,855 |
| 4-year College | -- | 13,000 N=1 | -- | -- | -- N=0 | -- | -- | -- N=0 | -- | -- | -- N=0 | -- | 10,667 | 16,679 N=6 | 22,628 | 28,470 | 29,511 N=2 | 30,552 |
| Univ. | 12,949 | 17,487 N=8 | 22,860 | 24,232 | 30,767 N=8 | 36,600 | 10,920 | 22,507 N=12 | 39,000 | 12,254 | 40,263 N=11 | 60,000 | 10,920 | 20,762 N=40 | 39,000 | 12,254 | 35,767 N=35 | 60,000 |
| All | 8,268 | 15,373 N=80 | 25,000 | 9,500 | 24,421 N=76 | 40,500 | 10,920 | 21,132 N=85 | 39,000 | 12,254 | 29,956 N=83 | 60,176 | 8,268 | 17,991 N=315 | 39,000 | 9,500 | 26,616 N=299 | 60,176 |

*Small public = public library serving a population of from 25,000 to 99,999.
**Large public = public library serving a population of over 100,000.

N = number of libraries

Source: ALA SURVEY OF LIBRARIAN SALARIES, 1984

Table 10B. Salaries Paid to Department Head/Branch Head by Type of Library and Region of the U.S. (in dollars)

| Region<br>Type of Library | North Atlantic | | | Great Lakes and Plains | | |
|---|---|---|---|---|---|---|
| | Low | Mean | High | Low | Mean | High |
| Small Public* | 8,000 | 18,558<br>N=99 | 33,190 | 8,081 | 17,937<br>N=118 | 39,146 |
| Large Public** | 13,000 | 23,638<br>N=175 | 36,816 | 10,500 | 22,770<br>N=397 | 42,492 |
| 2-year College | 19,694 | 26,897<br>N=4 | 40,999 | 14,500 | 28,121<br>N=4 | 39,702 |
| 4-year College | 18,000 | 24,802<br>N=10 | 30,745 | 9,840 | 18,502<br>N=10 | 26,580 |
| Univ. | 16,500 | 28,604<br>N=141 | 43,378 | 13,781 | 25,305<br>N=72 | 37,900 |
| All | 8,000 | 24,155<br>N=429 | 43,378 | 8,081 | 22,089<br>N=601 | 42,492 |

*Small public = public library serving a population of from 25,000 to 99,999.
**Large public = public library serving a population of over 100,000.

N = number of incumbents

Source: ALA SURVEY OF LIBRARIAN SALARIES, 1984

Table 10B.(cont.) Salaries Paid to Department Head/Branch Head by Type of Library and Region of the U.S. (in dollars)

| Region<br>Type of Library | Southeast | | | West and Southwest | | | All Libraries | | |
|---|---|---|---|---|---|---|---|---|---|
| | Low | Mean | High | Low | Mean | High | Low | Mean | High |
| Small Public* | 8,153 | 13,080<br>N=44 | 18,506 | 13,976 | 23,835<br>N=51 | 37,200 | 8,000 | 18,413<br>N=312 | 39,146 |
| Large Public** | 8,268 | 21,096<br>N=325 | 34,344 | 13,380 | 24,806<br>N=304 | 56,720 | 8,268 | 22,959<br>N=1201 | 56,720 |
| 2-year College | 21,768 | 28,410<br>N=8 | 34,759 | 11,500 | 33,349<br>N=8 | 44,272 | 11,500 | 29,756<br>N=24 | 44,272 |
| 4-year College | 16,300 | 19,448<br>N=10 | 22,176 | -- | --<br>N=0 | -- | 9,840 | 20,918<br>N=30 | 30,745 |
| Univ. | 14,980 | 24,073<br>N=109 | 41,334 | 12,979 | 27,971<br>N=169 | 51,000 | 12,979 | 26,896<br>N=491 | 51,000 |
| All | 8,153 | 21,124<br>N=496 | 41,334 | 11,500 | 25,847<br>N=532 | 56,720 | 8,000 | 23,259<br>N=2058 | 56,720 |

*Small public = public library serving a population of from 25,000 to 99,999.
**Large public = public library serving a population of over 100,000.

N = number of incumbents

Source: ALA SURVEY OF LIBRARIAN SALARIES, 1984

Table 11A. Scheduled Salaries for Reference/Information Librarian by Type of Library and Region of the U.S. (in dollars)

| Region | North Atlantic | | | | | | Great Lakes and Plains | | | | | |
|---|---|---|---|---|---|---|---|---|---|---|---|---|
| | Starting | | | Maximum | | | Starting | | | Maximum | | |
| Type of Library | Low | Mean | High | Low | Mean | High | Low | Mean | High | Low | Mean | High |
| Small Public* | 9,500 | 14,925 N=41 | 23,605 | 11,703 | 20,218 N=37 | 30,483 | 8,548 | 14,472 N=34 | 26,543 | 12,897 | 20,649 N=31 | 33,876 |
| Large Public** | 10,975 | 15,207 N=19 | 20,371 | 17,472 | 22,063 N=19 | 28,847 | 12,184 | 16,298 N=43 | 22,818 | 16,205 | 22,744 N=43 | 35,343 |
| 2-year College | 12,263 | 17,225 N=9 | 20,484 | 24,581 | 34,823 N=7 | 53,411 | 13,966 | 19,252 N=18 | 27,231 | 18,306 | 37,001 N=18 | 54,321 |
| 4-year College | 12,361 | 16,860 N=10 | 28,212 | 16,000 | 24,858 N=8 | 41,727 | -- | 11,000 N=1 | -- | -- | -- N=0 | -- |
| Univ. | 11,300 | 17,648 N=18 | 24,375 | 23,315 | 33,116 N=14 | 47,733 | 14,000 | 16,974 N=10 | 19,440 | 19,956 | 25,684 N=8 | 47,609 |
| All | 9,500 | 15,898 N=97 | 28,212 | 11,703 | 24,394 N=85 | 53,410 | 8,548 | 16,228 N=106 | 27,231 | 12,897 | 24,896 N=100 | 54,321 |

*Small public = public library serving a population of from 25,000 to 99,999.
**Large public = public library serving a population of over 100,000.

N = number of libraries

Source: ALA SURVEY OF LIBRARIAN SALARIES, 1984

Table 11A.(cont.) Scheduled Salaries for Reference/Information Librarian by Type of Library and Region of the U.S. (in dollars)

| Region | Southeast | | | | | | | West and Southwest | | | | | | | All Libraries | | | | | | |
|---|---|---|---|---|---|---|---|---|---|---|---|---|---|---|---|---|---|---|---|---|---|
| | Starting | | | Maximum | | | | Starting | | | Maximum | | | | Starting | | | Maximum | | | |
| Type of Library | Low | Mean | High | Low | Mean | High | | Low | Mean | High | Low | Mean | High | | Low | Mean | High | Low | Mean | High | |
| Small Public* | 8,000 | 13,711 N=19 | 16,246 | 8,500 | 19,606 N=17 | 23,481 | | 9,456 | 17,893 N=31 | 23,148 | 11,490 | 23,013 N=31 | 30,984 | | 8,000 | 15,353 N=125 | 26,543 | 8,500 | 20,990 N=116 | 33,876 | |
| Large Public** | 8,152 | 14,918 N=47 | 18,768 | 11,151 | 21,686 N=46 | 28,200 | | 13,200 | 18,539 N=45 | 25,616 | 16,812 | 24,060 N=44 | 34,272 | | 8,152 | 16,397 N=154 | 25,616 | 11,151 | 22,720 N=152 | 35,343 | |
| 2-year College | 14,000 | 18,360 N=10 | 21,993 | 24,387 | 31,798 N=9 | 38,000 | | 14,500 | 22,094 N=16 | 29,131 | 30,000 | 40,668 N=16 | 51,855 | | 18,306 | 36,933 N=50 | 29,130 | 18,306 | 36,933 N=50 | 54,321 | |
| 4-year College | 13,000 | 13,750 N=4 | 16,000 | -- | 24,000 N=1 | -- | | -- | 15,693 N=1 | -- | -- | 33,000 N=1 | -- | | 11,000 | 15,644 N=16 | 28,212 | 16,000 | 25,586 N=10 | 41,727 | |
| Univ. | 11,016 | 16,126 N=10 | 22,070 | 18,500 | 24,185 N=9 | 36,600 | | 13,056 | 18,078 N=16 | 28,000 | 19,399 | 35,407 N=13 | 52,000 | | 11,016 | 17,369 N=54 | 28,000 | 18,500 | 30,615 N=44 | 52,000 | |
| All | 8,000 | 15,128 N=90 | 22,070 | 8,500 | 22,667 N=82 | 38,000 | | 9,456 | 18,783 N=109 | 29,131 | 11,490 | 27,772 N=105 | 52,000 | | 8,000 | 16,595 N=402 | 29,131 | 8,500 | 25,102 N=372 | 54,321 | |

*Small public = public library serving a population of from 25,000 to 99,999.
**Large public = public library serving a population of over 100,000.

N = number of libraries

Source: ALA SURVEY OF LIBRARIAN SALARIES, 1984

Table 11B. Salaries Paid to Reference/Information Librarian by Type of Library and Region of the U.S. (in dollars)

| Region<br>Type of Library | North Atlantic | | | Great Lakes and Plains | | |
|---|---|---|---|---|---|---|
| | Low | Mean | High | Low | Mean | High |
| Small Public* | 9,500 | 18,026<br>N=83 | 30,430 | 9,372 | 16,616<br>N=81 | 32,463 |
| Large Public** | 8,583 | 19,081<br>N=128 | 28,847 | 12,043 | 20,215<br>N=300 | 35,343 |
| 2-year College | 17,696 | 27,997<br>N=22 | 39,204 | 10,400 | 29,664<br>N=30 | 43,600 |
| 4-year College | 14,755 | 20,818<br>N=17 | 41,727 | 11,547 | 17,634<br>N=18 | 28,200 |
| Univ. | 12,000 | 21,762<br>N=110 | 43,096 | 13,500 | 21,219<br>N=67 | 39,212 |
| All | 8,583 | 20,284<br>N=360 | 43,096 | 9,372 | 20,241<br>N=496 | 43,600 |

*Small public = public library serving a population of from 25,000 to 99,999.
**Large public = public library serving a population of over 100,000.

N = number of incumbents

Source: ALA SURVEY OF LIBRARIAN SALARIES, 1984

Table 11B.(cont.) Salaries Paid to Reference/
Information Librarian by Type of Library and
Region of the U.S. (in dollars)

| Region<br>Type of Library | Southeast | | | West and Southwest | | | All Libraries | | |
|---|---|---|---|---|---|---|---|---|---|
| | Low | Mean | High | Low | Mean | High | Low | Mean | High |
| Small Public* | 8,200 | 14,950<br>N=28 | 20,754 | 14,269 | 22,638<br>N=51 | 28,584 | 8,200 | 18,170<br>N=243 | 32,463 |
| Large Public** | 8,382 | 19,128<br>N=233 | 27,357 | 10,800 | 21,186<br>N=275 | 32,627 | 8,382 | 20,075<br>N=936 | 35,343 |
| 2-year College | 18,046 | 24,315<br>N=26 | 33,559 | 11,500 | 32,786<br>N=27 | 43,320 | 10,400 | 28,793<br>N=105 | 43,600 |
| 4-year College | 12,500 | 18,937<br>N=17 | 27,733 | 11,114 | 18,786<br>N=7 | 25,206 | 11,114 | 19,064<br>N=59 | 41,727 |
| Univ. | 11,016 | 18,729<br>N=109 | 30,025 | 12,000 | 23,740<br>N=202 | 38,172 | 11,016 | 21,829<br>N=488 | 43,096 |
| All | 8,200 | 19,058<br>N=413 | 33,559 | 10,800 | 22,763<br>N=562 | 43,320 | 8,200 | 20,757<br>N=1831 | 43,600 |

*Small public = public library serving a population of from 25,000 to 99,999.
**Large public = public library serving a population of over 100,000.

N = number of incumbents

Source: ALA SURVEY OF LIBRARIAN SALARIES, 1984

Table 12A. Scheduled Salaries for Cataloger and/or Classifier by Type of Library and Region of U.S. (in dollars)

| Region | North Atlantic | | | | | | Great Lakes and Plains | | | | | |
|---|---|---|---|---|---|---|---|---|---|---|---|---|
| | Starting | | | Maximum | | | Starting | | | Maximum | | |
| Type of Library | Low | Mean | High | Low | Mean | High | Low | Mean | High | Low | Mean | High |
| Small Public* | 11,325 | 15,331 N=21 | 23,605 | 14,000 | 20,748 N=20 | 30,595 | 8,256 | 14,359 N=24 | 22,048 | 12,220 | 19,956 N=22 | 29,830 |
| Large Public** | 10,500 | 16,398 N=17 | 29,348 | 16,598 | 23,368 N=17 | 37,263 | 9,395 | 15,520 N=38 | 22,293 | 12,958 | 21,527 N=38 | 35,343 |
| 2-year College | 10,302 | 15,365 N=8 | 19,591 | 15,615 | 31,961 N=6 | 53,411 | 13,500 | 17,811 N=12 | 25,123 | 15,000 | 32,092 N=12 | 54,321 |
| 4-year College | 10,883 | 16,753 N=10 | 22,751 | 13,350 | 24,171 N=9 | 34,918 | 11,000 | 14,079 N=3 | 20,037 | -- | 23,397 N=1 | -- |
| Univ. | 11,300 | 18,228 N=20 | 24,375 | 20,900 | 31,919 N=16 | 47,733 | 14,000 | 16,733 N=12 | 20,580 | 19,956 | 25,497 N=10 | 47,609 |
| All | 10,302 | 16,523 N=76 | 29,348 | 13,350 | 25,474 N=68 | 53,411 | 8,256 | 15,631 N=89 | 25,123 | 12,220 | 23,139 N=83 | 54,321 |

*Small public = public library serving a population of from 25,000 to 99,999.
**Large public = public library serving a population of over 100,000.

N = number of libraries

Source: ALA SURVEY OF LIBRARIAN SALARIES, 1984

Table 12A.(cont.) Scheduled Salaries for Cataloger and/or Classifier by Type of Library and Region of the U.S. (in dollars)

| Region | Southeast | | | | | | West and Southwest | | | | | | All Libraries | | | | | |
|---|---|---|---|---|---|---|---|---|---|---|---|---|---|---|---|---|---|---|
| | Starting | | | Maximum | | | Starting | | | Maximum | | | Starting | | | Maximum | | |
| Type of Library | Low | Mean | High | Low | Mean | High | Low | Mean | High | Low | Mean | High | Low | Mean | High | Low | Mean | High |
| Small Public* | 9,180 | 13,426 N=17 | 16,656 | 13,061 | 18,605 N=14 | 23,046 | 9,660 | 17,791 N=20 | 23,148 | 12,936 | 23,196 N=20 | 30,984 | 8,256 | 15,251 N=82 | 23,605 | 12,220 | 20,768 N=76 | 30,984 |
| Large Public** | 9,715 | 15,548 N=39 | 20,172 | 12,033 | 22,189 N=39 | 32,905 | 13,200 | 18,708 N=33 | 26,400 | 16,812 | 24,575 N=32 | 33,800 | 9,395 | 16,474 N=127 | 29,348 | 12,033 | 22,755 N=126 | 37,263 |
| 2-year College | 14,000 | 18,158 N=8 | 20,553 | 20,000 | 30,679 N=7 | 38,400 | 10,000 | 20,411 N=8 | 25,529 | 12,000 | 35,235 N=8 | 43,501 | 10,000 | 17,922 N=36 | 25,529 | 12,000 | 32,530 N=33 | 54,321 |
| 4-year College | 10,000 | 12,100 N=4 | 13,000 | -- | -- N=0 | -- | -- | -- N=0 | -- | -- | -- N=0 | -- | 10,000 | 15,186 N=17 | 22,751 | 13,350 | 24,093 N=10 | 34,918 |
| Univ. | 8,112 | 15,267 N=11 | 22,198 | 13,476 | 23,800 N=9 | 36,600 | 10,920 | 18,241 N=15 | 28,000 | 15,475 | 35,473 N=12 | 52,000 | 8,112 | 17,361 N=58 | 28,000 | 13,476 | 29,905 N=47 | 52,000 |
| All | 8,112 | 15,142 N=79 | 22,198 | 12,033 | 22,534 N=69 | 38,400 | 9,660 | 18,554 N=76 | 28,000 | 12,000 | 27,193 N=72 | 52,000 | 8,112 | 16,416 N=320 | 29,348 | 12,000 | 24,539 N=292 | 54,321 |

*Small public = public library serving a population of from 25,000 to 99,999.
**Large public = public library serving a population of over 100,000.

N = number of libraries

Source: ALA SURVEY OF LIBRARIAN SALARIES, 1984

Table 12B. Salaries Paid to Cataloger and/or Classifier by Type of Library and Region of the U.S. (in dollars)

| Region<br>Type of Library | North Atlantic | | | Great Lakes and Plains | | |
|---|---|---|---|---|---|---|
| | Low | Mean | High | Low | Mean | High |
| Small Public* | 12,209 | 19,080<br>N=26 | 31,113 | 8,190 | 15,875<br>N=35 | 23,940 |
| Large Public** | 12,949 | 20,239<br>N=35 | 31,831 | 12,231 | 19,316<br>N=69 | 35,343 |
| 2-year College | 10,000 | 19,411<br>N=10 | 31,433 | 10,400 | 23,515<br>N=14 | 39,702 |
| 4-year College | 10,500 | 19,096<br>N=19 | 30,552 | 11,000 | 18,135<br>N=16 | 33,900 |
| Univ. | 12,700 | 22,015<br>N=103 | 43,097 | 14,119 | 21,880<br>N=51 | 34,728 |
| All | 10,000 | 20,875<br>N=193 | 43,097 | 8,190 | 19,587<br>N=185 | 39,702 |

\*Small public = public library serving a population of from 25,000 to 99,999.
\*\*Large public = public library serving a population of over 100,000.

N = number of incumbents

Source: ALA SURVEY OF LIBRARIAN SALARIES, 1984

Table 12B.(cont.) Salaries Paid to Cataloger
and/or Classifier by Type of Library and
Region of the U.S. (in dollars)

| Region<br>Type of Library | Southeast | | | West and Southwest | | | All Libraries | | |
|---|---|---|---|---|---|---|---|---|---|
| | Low | Mean | High | Low | Mean | High | Low | Mean | High |
| Small Public* | 8,700 | 14,693<br>N=25 | 24,420 | 12,936 | 21,082<br>N=23 | 28,452 | 8,190 | 17,467<br>N=109 | 31,113 |
| Large Public** | 9,715 | 19,117<br>N=66 | 28,424 | 15,252 | 21,855<br>N=47 | 32,627 | 9,715 | 19,954<br>N=217 | 35,343 |
| 2-year College | 15,612 | 23,470<br>N=7 | 33,553 | 15,333 | 28,157<br>N=13 | 40,788 | 10,000 | 23,947<br>N=44 | 40,788 |
| 4-year College | 10,500 | 17,128<br>N=17 | 29,648 | 9,000 | 14,696<br>N=7 | 18,720 | 9,000 | 17,746<br>N=59 | 33,900 |
| Univ. | 10,138 | 18,852<br>N=64 | 27,995 | 10,920 | 23,160<br>N=132 | 38,172 | 10,138 | 21,849<br>N=350 | 43,097 |
| All | 8,700 | 18,386<br>N=179 | 33,553 | 9,000 | 22,694<br>N=222 | 40,788 | 8,190 | 20,516<br>N=779 | 43,097 |

 *Small public = public library serving a population of from 25,000 to 99,999.
**Large public = public library serving a population of over 100,000.

N = number of incumbents

Source:  ALA SURVEY OF LIBRARIAN SALARIES, 1984

Table 13A. Scheduled Salaries for Serials Librarian by Type of Library and Region of the U.S. (in dollars)

| Region | North Atlantic | | | | | | | Great Lakes and Plains | | | | | | |
|---|---|---|---|---|---|---|---|---|---|---|---|---|---|---|
| | Starting | | | Maximum | | | | Starting | | | | Maximum | | |
| Type of Library | Low | Mean | High | Low | Mean | High | | Low | Mean | High | | Low | Mean | High |
| Small Public* | 11,446 | 16,560 N=3 | 21,738 | 14,846 | 21,854 N=3 | 27,393 | | 8,548 | 13,521 N=3 | 22,929 | | 12,968 | 19,776 N=3 | 29,264 |
| Large Public** | 13,044 | 18,245 N=5 | 20,619 | 17,472 | 25,371 N=5 | 37,263 | | 9,922 | 17,139 N=8 | 23,179 | | 12,071 | 22,742 N=8 | 29,203 |
| 2-year College | -- | 16,092 N=1 | -- | -- | 47,754 N=1 | -- | | 10,219 | 12,525 N=2 | 14,831 | | 18,192 | 18,249 N=2 | 18,306 |
| 4-year College | 10,883 | 17,926 N=5 | 22,751 | 13,350 | 26,391 N=5 | 34,918 | | -- | 13,000 N=1 | -- | | -- | -- N=0 | -- |
| Univ. | 11,300 | 18,872 N=12 | 29,535 | 22,667 | 32,572 N=10 | 41,727 | | 14,500 | 18,153 N=8 | 23,101 | | 20,000 | 28,344 N=6 | 47,609 |
| All | 10,883 | 18,196 N=26 | 29,535 | 13,350 | 29,077 N=24 | 47,754 | | 8,548 | 16,407 N=22 | 23,179 | | 12,071 | 23,570 N=19 | 47,609 |

*Small public = public library serving a population of from 25,000 to 99,999.
**Large public = public library serving a population of over 100,000.

N = number of libraries

Source: ALA SURVEY OF LIBRARIAN SALARIES, 1984

Table 13A.(cont.) Scheduled Salaries for Serials Librarian by Type of Library and Region of the U.S. (in dollars)

| Region | Southeast | | | | | | West and Southwest | | | | | | All Libraries | | | | | |
|---|---|---|---|---|---|---|---|---|---|---|---|---|---|---|---|---|---|---|
| | Starting | | | Maximum | | | Starting | | | Maximum | | | Starting | | | Maximum | | |
| Type of Library | Low | Mean | High | Low | Mean | High | Low | Mean | High | Low | Mean | High | Low | Mean | High | Low | Mean | High |
| Small Public* | 9,724 | 11,362 N=2 | 13,000 | 13,624 | 14,062 N=2 | 14,500 | 9,539 | 11,712 N=3 | 14,196 | 12,878 | 14,541 N=3 | 17,064 | 8,548 | 13,464 N=11 | 22,929 | 12,878 | 17,876 N=11 | 29,264 |
| Large Public** | 9,362 | 14,327 N=10 | 18,033 | 11,680 | 19,103 N=10 | 22,609 | 13,200 | 18,399 N=13 | 26,400 | 16,626 | 24,449 N=12 | 33,800 | 9,362 | 16,967 N=36 | 26,400 | 11,680 | 22,663 N=35 | 37,263 |
| 2-year College | 13,600 | 17,283 N=5 | 20,553 | 20,000 | 31,759 N=4 | 38,400 | 19,220 | 20,020 N=2 | 20,820 | 36,100 | 37,676 N=2 | 39,252 | 10,219 | 16,760 N=10 | 20,820 | 18,192 | 31,849 N=9 | 47,754 |
| 4-year College | -- | 13,000 N=1 | -- | -- | -- N=0 | -- | -- | -- N=0 | -- | -- | -- N=0 | -- | 10,883 | 16,519 N=7 | 22,751 | 13,350 | 26,391 N=5 | 34,918 |
| Univ. | 13,116 | 15,994 N=7 | 18,500 | 20,800 | 25,094 N=5 | 36,600 | 10,920 | 19,631 N=9 | 28,000 | 15,475 | 34,423 N=9 | 45,000 | 10,920 | 18,342 N=36 | 29,535 | 15,475 | 31,036 N=30 | 47,609 |
| All | 9,362 | 15,095 N=25 | 20,553 | 11,680 | 22,460 N=21 | 38,400 | 9,539 | 18,187 N=27 | 28,000 | 12,878 | 27,776 N=26 | 45,000 | 8,548 | 17,025 N=100 | 29,535 | 11,680 | 25,995 N=90 | 47,754 |

*Small public = public library serving a population of from 25,000 to 99,999.
**Large public = public library serving a population of over 100,000.

N = number of libraries

Source: ALA SURVEY OF LIBRARIAN SALARIES, 1984

Table 13B. Salaries Paid to Serials Librarian by Type of Library and Region of the U.S. (in dollars)

| Region<br>Type of Library | North Atlantic | | | Great Lakes and Plains | | |
|---|---|---|---|---|---|---|
| | Low | Mean | High | Low | Mean | High |
| Small Public* | 14,170 | 17,822<br>N=3 | 22,799 | 10,706 | 15,989<br>N=4 | 25,279 |
| Large Public** | 10,296 | 21,309<br>N=8 | 37,263 | 11,080 | 18,065<br>N=9 | 26,478 |
| 2-year College | -- | 20,212<br>N=1 | -- | 10,912 | 12,572<br>N=4 | 15,994 |
| 4-year College | 10,991 | 19,171<br>N=7 | 34,499 | 10,483 | 14,041<br>N=5 | 16,800 |
| Univ. | 8,500 | 23,687<br>N=22 | 41,264 | 9,600 | 19,990<br>N=20 | 36,685 |
| All | 8,500 | 21,938<br>N=41 | 41,264 | 9,600 | 17,782<br>N=42 | 36,685 |

\*Small public = public library serving a population of from 25,000 to 99,999.
\*\*Large public = public library serving a population of over 100,000.

N = number of incumbents

Source: ALA SURVEY OF LIBRARIAN SALARIES, 1984

Table 13B.(cont.) Salaries Paid to Serials Librarian by Type of Library and Region of the U.S. (in dollars)

| Region | Southeast | | | West and Southwest | | | All Libraries | | |
|---|---|---|---|---|---|---|---|---|---|
| Type of Library | Low | Mean | High | Low | Mean | High | Low | Mean | High |
| Small Public* | 8,703 | 14,197 N=5 | 23,520 | 11,680 | 13,954 N=3 | 17,364 | 8,703 | 15,351 N=15 | 25,279 |
| Large Public** | 9,362 | 16,381 N=8 | 22,068 | 15,262 | 20,836 N=10 | 31,400 | 9,362 | 19,213 N=35 | 37,263 |
| 2-year College | 13,600 | 22,345 N=4 | 33,559 | 10,587 | 23,287 N=3 | 29,880 | 10,587 | 19,145 N=12 | 33,559 |
| 4-year College | 9,360 | 15,089 N=6 | 23,733 | -- | 14,200 N=1 | -- | 9,360 | 16,270 N=19 | 34,499 |
| Univ. | 15,000 | 20,723 N=27 | 33,496 | 12,257 | 22,202 N=20 | 39,000 | 8,500 | 21,624 N=89 | 41,264 |
| All | 8,703 | 18,830 N=50 | 33,559 | 10,587 | 21,036 N=37 | 39,000 | 8,500 | 19,801 N=170 | 41,264 |

*Small public = public library serving a population of from 25,000 to 99,999.
**Large public = public library serving a population of over 100,000.

N = number of incumbents

Source: ALA SURVEY OF LIBRARIAN SALARIES, 1984

Table 14A. Scheduled Salaries for Audiovisual Librarian by Type of Library and Region of the U.S. (in dollars)

| Region | North Atlantic | | | | | | Great Lakes and Plains | | | | | |
|---|---|---|---|---|---|---|---|---|---|---|---|---|
| | Starting | | | Maximum | | | Starting | | | Maximum | | |
| Type of Library | Low | Mean | High | Low | Mean | High | Low | Mean | High | Low | Mean | High |
| Small Public* | 12,148 | 16,537 N=6 | 23,547 | 15,846 | 21,343 N=6 | 30,595 | 10,005 | 15,987 N=10 | 22,929 | 12,085 | 21,379 N=10 | 29,264 |
| Large Public** | 9,984 | 16,915 N=14 | 27,347 | 13,692 | 22,774 N=14 | 37,853 | 9,022 | 17,623 N=24 | 25,116 | 10,977 | 23,893 N=24 | 32,240 |
| 2-year College | 10,302 | 15,382 N=5 | 19,591 | 23,171 | 31,937 N=5 | 53,411 | 11,594 | 17,526 N=9 | 22,096 | 18,165 | 33,777 N=9 | 54,321 |
| 4-year College | 13,332 | 16,758 N=7 | 20,876 | 16,355 | 25,151 N=5 | 28,749 | -- | 14,483 N=1 | -- | -- | -- N=0 | -- |
| Univ. | 11,300 | 18,375 N=8 | 24,473 | 25,200 | 33,207 N=7 | 41,000 | 8,000 | 15,705 N=6 | 20,000 | 14,000 | 26,063 N=5 | 47,609 |
| All | 9,984 | 16,931 N=40 | 27,347 | 13,692 | 26,075 N=37 | 53,411 | 8,000 | 16,985 N=50 | 25,116 | 10,977 | 25,449 N=48 | 54,321 |

*Small public = public library serving a population of from 25,000 to 99,999.
**Large public = public library serving a population of over 100,000.

N = number of libraries

Source: ALA SURVEY OF LIBRARIAN SALARIES, 1984

Table 14A.(cont.) Scheduled Salaries for Audiovisual Librarian by Type of Library and Region of the U.S. (in dollars)

| Region | Southeast | | | | | | West and Southwest | | | | | | All Libraries | | | | | |
|---|---|---|---|---|---|---|---|---|---|---|---|---|---|---|---|---|---|---|
| | Starting | | | Maximum | | | Starting | | | Maximum | | | Starting | | | Maximum | | |
| Type of Library | Low | Mean | High | Low | Mean | High | Low | Mean | High | Low | Mean | High | Low | Mean | High | Low | Mean | High |
| Small Public* | -- | 14,378 N=1 | -- | -- | 20,124 N=1 | -- | 14,652 | 19,379 N=8 | 31,616 | 18,744 | 25,048 N=8 | 37,586 | 10,005 | 17,140 N=25 | 31,616 | 12,085 | 22,494 N=25 | 37,586 |
| Large Public** | 11,040 | 16,339 N=22 | 26,917 | 12,600 | 22,652 N=22 | 39,768 | 13,200 | 19,484 N=21 | 27,008 | 17,496 | 25,389 N=20 | 36,192 | 9,022 | 17,634 N=81 | 27,347 | 10,977 | 23,730 N=80 | 39,768 |
| 2-year College | 10,080 | 17,547 N=10 | 24,227 | 15,905 | 27,422 N=7 | 38,400 | 10,000 | 19,354 N=5 | 25,167 | 12,000 | 34,255 N=5 | 51,855 | 10,000 | 17,479 N=29 | 25,167 | 12,000 | 31,804 N=26 | 54,321 |
| 4-year College | 13,000 | 14,500 N=2 | 16,000 | -- | 21,333 N=1 | -- | -- | -- N=0 | -- | -- | -- N=0 | -- | 13,000 | 16,079 N=10 | 20,876 | 16,355 | 24,515 N=6 | 28,749 |
| Univ. | 13,116 | 18,624 N=3 | 21,789 | 20,328 | 23,648 N=3 | 27,954 | 25,116 | 26,986 N=4 | 28,000 | 32,449 | 37,753 N=4 | 52,000 | 8,000 | 19,288 N=21 | 28,000 | 14,000 | 30,774 N=19 | 52,000 |
| All | 10,080 | 16,689 N=38 | 26,917 | 12,600 | 23,609 N=34 | 39,768 | 10,000 | 20,235 N=38 | 31,616 | 12,000 | 27,850 N=37 | 52,000 | 8,000 | 17,648 N=166 | 31,616 | 10,977 | 25,766 N=156 | 54,321 |

*Small public = public library serving a population of from 25,000 to 99,999.
**Large public = public library serving a population of over 100,000.

N = number of libraries

Source: ALA SURVEY OF LIBRARIAN SALARIES, 1984

Table 14B. Salaries Paid to Audiovisual Librarian by Type of Library and Region of the U.S. (in dollars)

| Region<br>Type of Library | North Atlantic | | | Great Lakes and Plains | | |
|---|---|---|---|---|---|---|
| | Low | Mean | High | Low | Mean | High |
| Small Public* | 14,372 | 20,375<br>N=8 | 30,595 | 8,957 | 15,186<br>N=21 | 29,264 |
| Large Public** | 8,697 | 20,090<br>N=15 | 41,364 | 10,267 | 21,027<br>N=25 | 32,240 |
| 2-year College | 15,300 | 24,013<br>N=7 | 41,003 | 10,200 | 22,359<br>N=13 | 40,752 |
| 4-year College | 11,200 | 19,000<br>N=10 | 29,131 | 10,165 | 18,039<br>N=8 | 26,225 |
| Univ. | 12,200 | 24,047<br>N=13 | 37,278 | 11,000 | 20,427<br>N=14 | 37,693 |
| All | 8,697 | 21,416<br>N=53 | 41,364 | 8,957 | 19,327<br>N=81 | 40,752 |

\*Small public = public library serving a population of from 25,000 to 99,999.
\*\*Large public = public library serving a population of over 100,000.

N = number of incumbents

Source: ALA SURVEY OF LIBRARIAN SALARIES, 1984

Table 14B.(cont.) Salaries Paid to Audiovisual Librarian by Type of Library and Region of the U.S. (in dollars)

| Region | Southeast | | | West and Southwest | | | All Libraries | | |
|---|---|---|---|---|---|---|---|---|---|
| Type of Library | Low | Mean | High | Low | Mean | High | Low | Mean | High |
| Small Public* | 10,231 | 12,305 N=2 | 14,378 | 15,276 | 20,235 N=7 | 24,516 | 8,957 | 17,057 N=38 | 30,595 |
| Large Public** | 11,040 | 19,953 N=26 | 29,404 | 15,252 | 23,243 N=18 | 32,686 | 8,697 | 21,002 N=84 | 41,364 |
| 2-year College | 15,415 | 21,731 N=11 | 33,559 | 15,333 | 27,556 N=7 | 42,054 | 10,200 | 23,439 N=38 | 42,054 |
| 4-year College | 9,568 | 17,556 N=9 | 27,867 | -- | 8,813 N=1 | -- | 8,813 | 17,897 N=28 | 29,131 |
| Univ. | 14,280 | 19,070 N=9 | 24,075 | 9,627 | 26,096 N=13 | 36,000 | 9,627 | 22,642 N=49 | 37,693 |
| All | 9,568 | 19,510 N=57 | 33,559 | 8,813 | 23,934 N=46 | 42,054 | 8,697 | 20,732 N=237 | 42,054 |

*Small public = public library serving a population of from 25,000 to 99,999.
**Large public = public library serving a population of over 100,000.

N = number of incumbents

Source: ALA SURVEY OF LIBRARIAN SALARIES, 1984

Table 15A. Scheduled Salaries for Government Documents Librarian by Type of Library and Region of the U.S. (in dollars)

| Region | North Atlantic | | | | | | Great Lakes and Plains | | | | | |
|---|---|---|---|---|---|---|---|---|---|---|---|---|
| | Starting | | | Maximum | | | Starting | | | Maximum | | |
| Type of Library | Low | Mean | High | Low | Mean | High | Low | Mean | High | Low | Mean | High |
| Small Public* | -- | 23,547 N=1 | -- | -- | 30,595 N=1 | -- | -- | 8,548 N=1 | -- | -- | 17,096 N=1 | -- |
| Large Public** | 12,500 | 17,784 N=6 | 26,150 | 17,890 | 24,344 N=6 | 30,000 | 10,920 | 17,848 N=14 | 27,196 | 15,520 | 24,693 N=14 | 34,918 |
| 2-year College | -- | N=0 | -- | -- | N=0 | -- | -- | N=0 | -- | -- | N=0 | -- |
| 4-year College | -- | N=0 | -- | -- | N=0 | -- | -- | N=0 | -- | -- | N=0 | -- |
| Univ. | 12,361 | 17,055 N=7 | 24,375 | 23,171 | 27,689 N=4 | 32,479 | 14,616 | 16,845 N=5 | 18,000 | 21,408 | 31,252 N=3 | 47,609 |
| All | 12,361 | 17,831 N=14 | 26,150 | 17,890 | 26,129 N=11 | 32,479 | 8,548 | 17,132 N=20 | 27,196 | 15,520 | 25,364 N=18 | 47,609 |

*Small public = public library serving a population of from 25,000 to 99,999.
**Large public = public library serving a population of over 100,000.

N = number of libraries

Source:  ALA SURVEY OF LIBRARIAN SALARIES, 1984

Table 15A.(cont.) Scheduled Salaries for Government Document Librarian by Type of Library and Region of the U.S. (in dollars)

| Region | Southeast | | | | | | West and Southwest | | | | | | All Libraries | | | | | |
|---|---|---|---|---|---|---|---|---|---|---|---|---|---|---|---|---|---|---|
| | Starting | | | Maximum | | | Starting | | | Maximum | | | Starting | | | Maximum | | |
| Type of Library | Low | Mean | High | Low | Mean | High | Low | Mean | High | Low | Mean | High | Low | Mean | High | Low | Mean | High |
| Small Public* | -- | -- N=0 | -- | -- | -- N=0 | -- | -- | 15,671 N=1 | -- | -- | 19,048 N=1 | -- | 8,548 | 15,922 N=3 | 23,547 | 17,096 | 22,246 N=3 | 30,595 |
| Large Public** | 11,600 | 16,587 N=14 | 26,295 | 16,000 | 22,412 N=14 | 29,985 | 13,200 | 19,206 N=21 | 22,980 | 16,812 | 24,450 N=20 | 30,942 | 10,920 | 18,039 N=55 | 27,196 | 15,520 | 23,973 N=54 | 34,918 |
| 2-year College | -- | -- N=0 | -- | -- | -- N=0 | -- | -- | -- N=0 | -- | -- | -- N=0 | -- | -- | -- N=0 | -- | -- | -- N=0 | -- |
| 4-year College | -- | -- N=0 | -- | -- | -- N=0 | -- | -- | -- N=0 | -- | -- | -- N=0 | -- | -- | -- N=0 | -- | -- | -- N=0 | -- |
| Univ. | 15,000 | 16,980 N=3 | 18,660 | 28,140 | 31,947 N=3 | 36,600 | 16,176 | 19,821 N=7 | 26,915 | 30,672 | 37,589 N=6 | 42,648 | 12,361 | 17,877 N=22 | 26,915 | 21,408 | 32,868 N=16 | 47,609 |
| All | 11,600 | 16,657 N=17 | 26,295 | 16,000 | 24,094 N=17 | 36,600 | 13,200 | 19,232 N=29 | 26,915 | 16,812 | 27,170 N=27 | 42,648 | 8,548 | 17,915 N=80 | 27,196 | 15,520 | 25,852 N=73 | 47,609 |

*Small public = public library serving a population of from 25,000 to 99,999.
**Large public = public library serving a population of over 100,000.

N = number of libraries

Source: ALA SURVEY OF LIBRARIAN SALARIES, 1984

Table 15B. Salaries Paid to Government Documents Librarian by Type of Library and Region of the U.S. (in dollars)

| Region | North Atlantic | | | Great Lakes and Plains | | |
|---|---|---|---|---|---|---|
| Type of Library | Low | Mean | High | Low | Mean | High |
| Small Public* | -- | 30,595<br>N=1 | -- | 12,260 | 12,732<br>N=2 | 13,204 |
| Large Public** | 12,750 | 21,258<br>N=6 | 30,000 | 12,043 | 20,689<br>N=18 | 34,918 |
| 2-year College | -- | --<br>N=0 | -- | -- | --<br>N=0 | -- |
| 4-year College | 13,800 | 14,400<br>N=2 | 15,000 | -- | 31,620<br>N=1 | -- |
| Univ. | 16,500 | 21,860<br>N=12 | 35,369 | 17,167 | 22,252<br>N=16 | 29,029 |
| All | 12,750 | 21,393<br>N=21 | 35,369 | 12,043 | 21,230<br>N=37 | 34,918 |

*Small public = public library serving a population of from 25,000 to 99,999.
**Large public = public library serving a population of over 100,000.

N = number of incumbents

Source: ALA SURVEY OF LIBRARIAN SALARIES, 1984

Table 15B.(cont.) Salaries Paid to Government Documents Librarian by Type of Library and Region of the U.S. (in dollars)

| Region<br>Type of Library | Southeast | | | West and Southwest | | | All Libraries | | |
|---|---|---|---|---|---|---|---|---|---|
| | Low | Mean | High | Low | Mean | High | Low | Mean | High |
| Small Public* | -- | 9,396<br>N=1 | -- | -- | 19,048<br>N=1 | -- | 9,396 | 16,901<br>N=5 | 30,595 |
| Large Public** | 14,518 | 18,714<br>N=14 | 28,260 | 13,929 | 22,368<br>N=17 | 30,942 | 12,043 | 20,767<br>N=55 | 34,918 |
| 2-year College | -- | --<br>N=0 | -- | -- | --<br>N=0 | -- | -- | --<br>N=0 | -- |
| 4-year College | -- | 14,450<br>N=1 | -- | -- | --<br>N=0 | -- | 13,800 | 18,718<br>N=4 | 31,620 |
| Univ. | 14,004 | 20,405<br>N=18 | 28,413 | 10,995 | 22,939<br>N=28 | 32,484 | 10,995 | 21,999<br>N=74 | 35,369 |
| All | 9,396 | 19,210<br>N=34 | 28,413 | 10,995 | 22,643<br>N=46 | 32,484 | 9,396 | 21,228<br>N=138 | 35,369 |

*Small public = public library serving a population of from 25,000 to 99,999.
**Large public = public library serving a population of over 100,000.

N = number of incumbents

Source: ALA SURVEY OF LIBRARIAN SALARIES, 1984

Table 16A. Scheduled Salaries for Subject Specialist/Bibliographer by Type of Library and Region of the U.S. (in dollars)

| Region | North Atlantic | | | | | | Great Lakes and Plains | | | | | |
|---|---|---|---|---|---|---|---|---|---|---|---|---|
| | Starting | | | Maximum | | | Starting | | | Maximum | | |
| Type of Library | Low | Mean | High | Low | Mean | High | Low | Mean | High | Low | Mean | High |
| Small Public* | -- | 23,547 N=1 | -- | -- | 30,595 N=1 | -- | 10,863 | 15,734 N=4 | 22,929 | 16,082 | 21,097 N=4 | 29,264 |
| Large Public** | 14,148 | 16,431 N=5 | 20,371 | 18,960 | 23,272 N=5 | 26,673 | 14,500 | 19,153 N=10 | 33,280 | 21,000 | 25,828 N=10 | 44,590 |
| 2-year College | -- | 17,453 N=1 | -- | -- | 33,350 N=1 | -- | -- | -- N=0 | -- | -- | -- N=0 | -- |
| 4-year College | 14,715 | 18,433 N=4 | 21,650 | 23,937 | 29,108 N=3 | 34,918 | -- | -- N=0 | -- | -- | -- N=0 | -- |
| Univ. | 11,300 | 16,577 N=5 | 24,373 | 25,200 | 33,661 N=4 | 39,412 | 14,000 | 17,459 N=5 | 20,580 | 24,999 | 28,700 N=3 | 30,958 |
| All | 11,300 | 17,485 N=16 | 24,373 | 18,960 | 28,734 N=14 | 39,412 | 10,863 | 17,987 N=19 | 33,280 | 16,082 | 25,222 N=17 | 44,590 |

*Small public = public library serving a population of from 25,000 to 99,999.
**Large public = public library serving a population of over 100,000.

N = number of libraries

Source: ALA SURVEY OF LIBRARIAN SALARIES, 1984

Table 16A.(cont.)  Scheduled Salaries for Subject Specialist/Bibliographer by Type of Library and Region of the U.S. (in dollars)

| Region | Southeast | | | | | | West and Southwest | | | | | | All Libraries | | | | | |
|---|---|---|---|---|---|---|---|---|---|---|---|---|---|---|---|---|---|---|
| | Starting | | | Maximum | | | Starting | | | Maximum | | | Starting | | | Maximum | | |
| Type of Library | Low | Mean | High | Low | Mean | High | Low | Mean | High | Low | Mean | High | Low | Mean | High | Low | Mean | High |
| Small Public* | -- | -- N=0 | -- | -- | -- N=0 | -- | -- | 15,540 N=1 | -- | -- | 18,012 N=1 | -- | 10,863 | 17,004 N=6 | 23,547 | 16,082 | 22,166 N=6 | 30,595 |
| Large Public** | 15,564 | 18,631 N=6 | 20,795 | 20,856 | 26,645 N=6 | 31,091 | 12,763 | 19,416 N=12 | 25,616 | 15,954 | 25,815 N=11 | 34,272 | 12,763 | 18,742 N=33 | 33,280 | 15,594 | 25,577 N=32 | 44,590 |
| 2-year College | -- | -- N=0 | -- | -- | -- N=0 | -- | -- | 17,649 N=1 | -- | -- | 35,898 N=1 | -- | 17,453 | 17,551 N=2 | 17,649 | 33,350 | 34,624 N=2 | 35,898 |
| 4-year College | -- | -- N=0 | -- | -- | -- N=0 | -- | -- | -- N=0 | -- | -- | -- N=0 | -- | 14,715 | 18,433 N=4 | 21,650 | 23,937 | 29,108 N=3 | 34,918 |
| Univ. | 15,000 | 17,983 N=2 | 20,966 | 27,954 | 32,277 N=2 | 36,600 | 16,176 | 18,776 N=6 | 22,560 | 30,672 | 37,799 N=6 | 42,648 | 11,300 | 17,711 N=18 | 24,373 | 24,999 | 34,139 N=15 | 42,648 |
| All | 15,000 | 18,469 N=8 | 20,966 | 20,856 | 28,053 N=8 | 36,600 | 12,763 | 18,942 N=20 | 25,616 | 15,594 | 29,719 N=19 | 42,648 | 10,863 | 18,224 N=63 | 33,280 | 15,594 | 27,933 N=58 | 44,590 |

*Small public = public library serving a population of from 25,000 to 99,999.
**Large public = public library serving a population of over 100,000.

N = number of libraries

Source:  ALA SURVEY OF LIBRARIAN SALARIES, 1984

Table 16B. Salaries Paid to Subject Specialist/Bibliographer by Type of Library and Region of the U.S. (in dollars)

| Region<br>Type of Library | North Atlantic | | | Great Lakes and Plains | | |
|---|---|---|---|---|---|---|
| | Low | Mean | High | Low | Mean | High |
| Small Public* | -- | 30,595<br>N=1 | -- | 12,709 | 15,751<br>N=3 | 17,653 |
| Large Public** | 15,852 | 21,703<br>N=11 | 27,327 | 16,080 | 22,467<br>N=27 | 42,458 |
| 2-year College | 30,092 | 33,868<br>N=3 | 37,235 | -- | --<br>N=0 | -- |
| 4-year College | 10,500 | 20,669<br>N=4 | 32,004 | -- | 31,033<br>N=1 | -- |
| Univ. | 15,786 | 24,308<br>N=31 | 35,369 | 13,500 | 22,211<br>N=34 | 42,000 |
| All | 10,500 | 24,143<br>N=50 | 37,235 | 12,709 | 22,155<br>N=65 | 42,458 |

\*Small public = public library serving a population of from 25,000 to 99,999.
\*\*Large public = public library serving a population of over 100,000.

N = number of incumbents

Source: ALA SURVEY OF LIBRARIAN SALARIES, 1984

Table 16B.(cont.) Salaries Paid to Subject Specialist/Bibliographer by Type of Library and Region of the U.S. (in dollars)

| Region<br>Type of Library | Southeast | | | West and Southwest | | | All Libraries | | |
|---|---|---|---|---|---|---|---|---|---|
| | Low | Mean | High | Low | Mean | High | Low | Mean | High |
| Small Public* | -- | --<br>N=0 | -- | -- | 19,836<br>N=1 | -- | 12,709 | 19,537<br>N=5 | 30,595 |
| Large Public** | 16,275 | 23,103<br>N=7 | 28,556 | 14,596 | 25,008<br>N=43 | 28,606 | 14,596 | 23,664<br>N=88 | 42,458 |
| 2-year College | -- | --<br>N=0 | -- | -- | 23,514<br>N=1 | -- | 23,514 | 31,280<br>N=4 | 37,235 |
| 4-year College | 13,000 | 19,133<br>N=3 | 25,400 | -- | --<br>N=0 | -- | 10,500 | 21,389<br>N=8 | 32,004 |
| Univ. | 14,988 | 22,456<br>N=21 | 32,999 | 13,548 | 24,055<br>N=60 | 37,620 | 13,500 | 23,449<br>N=146 | 42,000 |
| All | 13,000 | 22,281<br>N=31 | 32,999 | 13,548 | 24,400<br>N=105 | 37,620 | 10,500 | 23,506<br>N=251 | 42,458 |

*Small public = public library serving a population of from 25,000 to 99,999.
**Large public = public library serving a population of over 100,000.

N = number of incumbents

Source:  ALA SURVEY OF LIBRARIAN SALARIES, 1984

Table 17A. Scheduled Salaries for Coordinator of Adult and/or Young Adult and/or Children's Services by Type of Library and Region of the U.S. (in dollars)

Region: North Atlantic

| Type of Library | Starting Low | Starting Mean | Starting High | Maximum Low | Maximum Mean | Maximum High |
|---|---|---|---|---|---|---|
| Small Public* | 10,518 | 15,243 N=9 | 21,738 | 13,177 | 21,197 N=8 | 27,471 |
| Large Public** | 12,500 | 19,829 N=13 | 27,347 | 16,969 | 26,205 N=13 | 37,853 |
| All | 10,518 | 17,953 N=22 | 27,347 | 13,177 | 24,297 N=21 | 37,853 |

Region: Great Lakes and Plains

| Type of Library | Starting Low | Starting Mean | Starting High | Maximum Low | Maximum Mean | Maximum High |
|---|---|---|---|---|---|---|
| Small Public* | 8,715 | 14,429 N=4 | 21,502 | 11,211 | 18,619 N=3 | 30,108 |
| Large Public** | 14,604 | 20,257 N=20 | 30,490 | 19,572 | 27,511 N=20 | 39,783 |
| All | 8,715 | 19,285 N=24 | 30,490 | 11,211 | 26,351 N=23 | 39,783 |

Region: Southeast

| Type of Library | Starting Low | Starting Mean | Starting High | Maximum Low | Maximum Mean | Maximum High |
|---|---|---|---|---|---|---|
| Small Public* | 10,769 | 12,087 N=2 | 13,404 | 13,745 | 16,341 N=2 | 18,936 |
| Large Public** | 13,500 | 17,899 N=17 | 26,917 | 17,500 | 24,846 N=17 | 39,768 |
| All | 10,769 | 17,287 N=19 | 26,917 | 13,745 | 23,950 N=19 | 39,768 |

Region: West and Southwest

| Type of Library | Starting Low | Starting Mean | Starting High | Maximum Low | Maximum Mean | Maximum High |
|---|---|---|---|---|---|---|
| Small Public* | 13,500 | 18,825 N=7 | 25,000 | 17,628 | 24,404 N=7 | 31,737 |
| Large Public** | 15,912 | 22,745 N=28 | 29,378 | 20,484 | 28,383 N=28 | 37,300 |
| All | 13,500 | 21,961 N=35 | 29,378 | 17,628 | 27,588 N=35 | 37,300 |

All Libraries

| Type of Library | Starting Low | Starting Mean | Starting High | Maximum Low | Maximum Mean | Maximum High |
|---|---|---|---|---|---|---|
| Small Public* | 8,715 | 15,948 N=22 | 25,000 | 11,211 | 21,447 N=20 | 31,737 |
| Large Public** | 12,500 | 20,564 N=78 | 30,490 | 16,969 | 27,025 N=78 | 39,783 |
| All | 8,715 | 19,549 N=100 | 30,490 | 11,211 | 25,887 N=98 | 39,783 |

*Small public = public library serving a population of from 25,000 to 99,999.
**Large public = public library serving a population of over 100,000.

N = number of libraries

Source: ALA SURVEY OF LIBRARIAN SALARIES, 1984

17B. Salaries Paid to Children's and/or Young
Adult Services Librarian by Type of Library and
Region of the U.S. (in dollars)

| Region / Type of Library | North Atlantic | | | Great Lakes and Plains | | |
|---|---|---|---|---|---|---|
| | Low | Mean | High | Low | Mean | High |
| Small Public* | 8,100 | 17,420 N=57 | 30,430 | 9,425 | 16,988 N=51 | 28,170 |
| Large Public** | 12,190 | 18,415 N=85 | 27,505 | 11,280 | 19,132 N=151 | 29,042 |
| All | 8,100 | 18,175 N=144 | 30,430 | 9,425 | 18,568 N=204 | 29,042 |

| Region / Type of Library | Southeast | | | West and Southwest | | | All Libraries | | |
|---|---|---|---|---|---|---|---|---|---|
| | Low | Mean | High | Low | Mean | High | Low | Mean | High |
| Small Public* | 8,058 | 13,353 N=33 | 21,792 | 10,500 | 20,675 N=33 | 28,584 | 8,058 | 17,139 N=174 | 30,430 |
| Large Public** | 9,722 | 17,107 N=100 | 29,808 | 11,844 | 19,795 N=105 | 30,942 | 9,722 | 18,693 N=441 | 30,942 |
| All | 8,058 | 16,300 N=134 | 32,896 | 10,500 | 20,028 N=139 | 30,942 | 8,058 | 18,314 N=621 | 32,896 |

*Small public = public library serving a population of from 25,000 to 99,999.
**Large public = public library serving a population of over 100,000.

N = number of incumbents

Source: ALA SURVEY OF LIBRARIAN SALARIES, 1984

Table 18A. Scheduled Salaries for Children's Librarians
by Type of Library and Region of the U.S. (in dollars)

## North Atlantic

| Region | | | | | | |
|---|---|---|---|---|---|---|
| | Starting | | | Maximum | | |
| Type of Library | Low | Mean | High | Low | Mean | High |
| Small Public* | 10,518 | 15,485 N=39 | 23,605 | 12,480 | 20,720 N=35 | 30,595 |
| Large Public** | 9,850 | 15,221 N=17 | 18,721 | 14,827 | 21,542 N=17 | 24,882 |
| All | 9,850 | 15,483 N=58 | 23,605 | 12,480 | 21,052 N=53 | 30,595 |

## Great Lakes and Plains

| Region | | | | | | |
|---|---|---|---|---|---|---|
| | Starting | | | Maximum | | |
| Type of Library | Low | Mean | High | Low | Mean | High |
| Small Public* | 9,087 | 15,350 N=30 | 22,929 | 12,968 | 20,475 N=29 | 29,830 |
| Large Public** | 12,000 | 16,011 N=29 | 21,434 | 14,824 | 23,271 N=29 | 37,052 |
| All | 9,087 | 15,675 N=59 | 22,929 | 12,968 | 21,873 N=58 | 37,052 |

## Southeast

| Region | | | | | | |
|---|---|---|---|---|---|---|
| | Starting | | | Maximum | | |
| Type of Library | Low | Mean | High | Low | Mean | High |
| Small Public* | 8,259 | 13,203 N=24 | 15,889 | 11,024 | 18,823 N=21 | 23,046 |
| Large Public** | 9,722 | 14,877 N=38 | 22,272 | 12,845 | 21,781 N=37 | 31,091 |
| All | 8,259 | 14,330 N=63 | 22,272 | 11,024 | 20,928 N=59 | 33,559 |

## West and Southwest

| Region | | | | | | |
|---|---|---|---|---|---|---|
| | Starting | | | Maximum | | |
| Type of Library | Low | Mean | High | Low | Mean | High |
| Small Public* | 9,660 | 18,396 N=28 | 34,091 | 12,763 | 23,715 N=28 | 40,664 |
| Large Public** | 12,082 | 18,265 N=40 | 24,348 | 17,139 | 23,557 N=39 | 30,942 |
| All | 9,660 | 18,319 N=68 | 34,091 | 12,763 | 23,623 N=67 | 40,664 |

## All Libraries

| | Starting | | | Maximum | | |
|---|---|---|---|---|---|---|
| Type of Library | Low | Mean | High | Low | Mean | High |
| Small Public* | 8,259 | 15,672 N=121 | 34,091 | 11,024 | 21,047 N=113 | 40,664 |
| Large Public** | 9,722 | 16,282 N=124 | 24,348 | 12,845 | 22,670 N=122 | 37,052 |
| All | 8,259 | 16,013 N=248 | 34,091 | 11,024 | 21,949 N=237 | 40,664 |

*Small public = public library serving a population of from 25,000 to 99,999.
**Large public = public library serving a population of over 100,000.

N = number of libraries

Source: ALA SURVEY OF LIBRARIAN SALARIES, 1984

18B. Salaries Paid to Adult Services Librarian
by Type of Library and Region of the U.S.
(in dollars)

| Region | North Atlantic | | | Great Lakes and Plains | | |
|---|---|---|---|---|---|---|
| Type of Library | Low | Mean | High | Low | Mean | High |
| Small Public* | 11,700 | 18,901 N=33 | 27,836 | 9,339 | 16,730 N=22 | 23,300 |
| Large Public** | 12,000 | 21,958 N=36 | 27,917 | 11,880 | 20,752 N=62 | 28,764 |
| All | 11,700 | 20,496 N=69 | 27,917 | 9,339 | 19,648 N=85 | 28,764 |

| Region | Southeast | | | West and Southwest | | | All Libraries | | |
|---|---|---|---|---|---|---|---|---|---|
| Type of Library | Low | Mean | High | Low | Mean | High | Low | Mean | High |
| Small Public* | 10,000 | 13,094 N=10 | 17,075 | 11,459 | 18,733 N=6 | 29,016 | 9,339 | 17,396 N=71 | 29,016 |
| Large Public** | 12,646 | 19,809 N=42 | 32,905 | 15,654 | 22,096 N=26 | 28,910 | 11,880 | 20,985 N=166 | 32,905 |
| All | 10,000 | 18,517 N=52 | 32,905 | 11,459 | 21,331 N=33 | 29,016 | 9,339 | 19,879 N=239 | 32,905 |

*Small public = public library serving a population of from 25,000 to 99,999.
**Large public = public library serving a population of over 100,000.

N = number of incumbents

Source: ALA SURVEY OF LIBRARIAN SALARIES, 1984

Table 19A. Scheduled Salaries for Adult Services Librarians by Type of Library and Region of the U.S. (in dollars)

| Region | | North Atlantic | | | | | | Great Lakes and Plains | | | | | |
|---|---|---|---|---|---|---|---|---|---|---|---|---|---|
| | | Starting | | | Maximum | | | Starting | | | Maximum | | |
| Type of Library | | Low | Mean | High | Low | Mean | High | Low | Mean | High | Low | Mean | High |
| Small Public* | | 10,000 | 15,827 N=20 | 25,542 | 14,000 | 21,837 N=16 | 33,190 | 8,715 | 16,165 N=13 | 22,048 | 11,211 | 21,293 N=13 | 29,830 |
| Large Public** | | 10,500 | 16,702 N=10 | 22,795 | 16,598 | 22,985 N=10 | 27,505 | 12,000 | 17,003 N=19 | 24,502 | 15,800 | 24,515 N=19 | 35,343 |
| All | | 10,000 | 16,119 N=30 | 25,542 | 14,000 | 22,278 N=26 | 33,190 | 8,715 | 16,663 N=32 | 24,502 | 11,211 | 23,205 N=32 | 35,343 |

| Region | Southeast | | | | | | West and Southwest | | | | | | All Libraries | | | | | |
|---|---|---|---|---|---|---|---|---|---|---|---|---|---|---|---|---|---|---|
| | Starting | | | Maximum | | | Starting | | | Maximum | | | Starting | | | Maximum | | |
| Type of Library | Low | Mean | High | Low | Mean | High | Low | Mean | High | Low | Mean | High | Low | Mean | High | Low | Mean | High |
| Small Public* | 8,259 | 13,033 N=9 | 17,075 | 11,619 | 18,498 N=8 | 24,025 | 10,014 | 15,708 N=5 | 23,213 | 14,910 | 20,627 N=5 | 29,016 | 8,259 | 15,373 N=47 | 25,542 | 11,211 | 20,888 N=42 | 33,190 |
| Large Public** | 12,000 | 16,830 N=20 | 22,271 | 16,931 | 23,732 N=20 | 34,344 | 15,199 | 19,422 N=17 | 23,767 | 20,916 | 24,894 N=17 | 29,547 | 10,500 | 17,528 N=66 | 24,502 | 15,800 | 24,143 N=66 | 35,343 |
| All | 8,259 | 15,652 N=29 | 22,271 | 11,619 | 22,237 N=28 | 34,344 | 10,014 | 18,365 N=23 | 23,767 | 14,910 | 23,776 N=23 | 29,547 | 8,259 | 16,606 N=114 | 25,542 | 11,211 | 22,856 N=109 | 35,343 |

*Small public = public library serving a population of from 25,000 to 99,999.
**Large public = public library serving a population of over 100,000.

N = number of libraries

Source: ALA SURVEY OF LIBRARIAN SALARIES, 1984

19B. Salaries Paid to Coordinator, Adult and/or Young Adult and/or Children's Services by Type of Library and Region of the U.S. (in dollars)

| Region | North Atlantic | | | Great Lakes and Plains | | |
|---|---|---|---|---|---|---|
| Type of Library | Low | Mean | High | Low | Mean | High |
| Small Public* | 12,176 | 19,851 N=9 | 26,277 | 9,339 | 16,892 N=4 | 21,502 |
| Large Public** | 15,392 | 25,459 N=16 | 42,605 | 18,075 | 25,108 N=26 | 32,240 |
| All | 12,176 | 23,440 N=25 | 42,605 | 9,339 | 24,013 N=30 | 32,240 |

| Region | Southeast | | | West and Southwest | | | All Libraries | | |
|---|---|---|---|---|---|---|---|---|---|
| Type of Library | Low | Mean | High | Low | Mean | High | Low | Mean | High |
| Small Public* | 13,500 | 13,896 N=3 | 14,688 | 18,333 | 22,780 N=6 | 31,737 | 9,339 | 19,300 N=22 | 31,737 |
| Large Public** | 13,500 | 22,551 N=21 | 34,354 | 17,283 | 27,348 N=39 | 36,477 | 13,500 | 25,493 N=102 | 42,605 |
| All | 13,500 | 21,469 N=24 | 34,354 | 17,283 | 26,739 N=45 | 36,477 | 9,339 | 24,394 N=124 | 42,605 |

*Small public = public library serving a population of from 25,000 to 99,999.
**Large public = public library serving a population of over 100,000.

N = number of incumbents

Source: ALA SURVEY OF LIBRARIAN SALARIES, 1984

## Employee Benefits

Table 20 summarizes responses to question E in Part I of the questionnaire. This question asked for:

Total employee benefits as a percent of total payroll. [Add up the total of what you pay in a year for all benefits you provide to ALL library employees (professional, support, others) and divide this total by the amount of your total yearly payroll.]

Table 20 shows the range of total employee benefits as a percent of total payroll for each of the twenty groups of libraries. The lowest, highest and mean percentage is given for each group.

Table 20 shows responses from libraries that gave a percentage. If the number seemed unusually low (under four percent) or unusually high (over forty percent) the respondent was called. In most cases a mathematical or conceptual difficulty was uncovered but these could not always be resolved in a way which yielded more than an approximate figure.

## Beginning Professionals

Question F on the questionnaire asked:

Within the last 12 months has the library hired any full time professional(s) with a master's degree in library science but no professional experience?

Question G asked the respondent to list annual salaries paid to all such persons. Table 21 shows the high, low and mean salary paid to beginning professionals in each of the twenty groups.

Table 20. Employee Benefits as a Percentage of Total Payroll by Type of Library and Region of the U.S.

| Region<br>Type of Library | North Atlantic | | | Great Lakes and Plains | | |
|---|---|---|---|---|---|---|
| | Low | Mean | High | Low | Mean | High |
| Small Public* | 2% | 17.2%<br>N=55 | 35% | 2% | 20.4%<br>N=60 | 72% |
| Large Public** | 7% | 20.6%<br>N=19 | 34% | 8% | 20.7%<br>N=43 | 44% |
| 2-year College | 18% | 26.8%<br>N=15 | 40% | 2% | 17.6%<br>N=36 | 31% |
| 4-year College | 1% | 19.4%<br>N=18 | 31% | 1% | 14.8%<br>N=24 | 30% |
| Univ. | 1% | 21.2%<br>N=33 | 40% | 4% | 19.6%<br>N=34 | 57% |
| All | 1% | 19.9%<br>N=140 | 40% | 1% | 19.1%<br>N=197 | 72% |

*Small public = public library serving a population of from 25,000 to 99,999.
**Large public = public library serving a population of over 100,000.

N = number of incumbents

Source: ALA SURVEY OF LIBRARIAN SALARIES, 1984

Table 20. (cont.) Employee Benefits as a Percentage of Total Payroll by Type of Library and Region of the U.S.

| Region<br>Type of Library | Southeast | | | West and Southwest | | | All Libraries | | |
|---|---|---|---|---|---|---|---|---|---|
| | Low | Mean | High | Low | Mean | High | Low | Mean | High |
| Small Public* | 1% | 16.4%<br>N=59 | 56% | 9% | 22.5%<br>N=42 | 40% | 1% | 18.9%<br>N=216 | 72% |
| Large Public** | 2% | 18.2%<br>N=52 | 35% | 8% | 21.4%<br>N=49 | 35% | 2% | 20.1%<br>N=163 | 44% |
| 2-year College | 3% | 17.4%<br>N=32 | 28% | 5% | 21.8%<br>N=34 | 47% | 2% | 20.0%<br>N=117 | 47% |
| 4-year College | 5% | 16.6%<br>N=21 | 22% | 3% | 12.1%<br>N=15 | 20% | 1% | 15.8%<br>N=78 | 31% |
| Univ. | 3% | 15.7%<br>N=30 | 45% | 6% | 20.2%<br>N=38 | 32% | 1% | 19.3%<br>N=135 | 57% |
| All | 1% | 16.9%<br>N=194 | 56% | 3% | 20.7%<br>N=178 | 47% | 1% | 19.1%<br>N=709 | 72% |

*Small public = public library serving a population of from 25,000 to 99,999.
**Large public = public library serving a population of over 100,000.

N = number of incumbents

Source: ALA SURVEY OF LIBRARIAN SALARIES, 1984

Table 21. Salaries Paid to Beginning Professionals by Type of Library and Region of the U.S. (in dollars)

| Region<br>Type of Library | North Atlantic | | | Great Lakes and Plains | | |
|---|---|---|---|---|---|---|
| | Low | Mean | High | Low | Mean | High |
| Small Public* | 12,500 | 15,183<br>N=11 | 23,000 | 11,000 | 14,659<br>N=12 | 19,807 |
| Large Public** | 10,500 | 14,727<br>N=36 | 18,721 | 11,398 | 15,588<br>N=36 | 21,434 |
| 2-year College | -- | 16,843<br>N=1 | -- | 13,500 | 17,765<br>N=5 | 24,000 |
| 4-year College | 13,422 | 22,672<br>N=11 | 33,773 | 9,000 | 14,119<br>N=8 | 17,077 |
| Univ. | 13,000 | 15,173<br>N=8 | 17,000 | 13,500 | 15,360<br>N=9 | 18,000 |
| All | 10,500 | 16,191<br>N=67 | 33,773 | 9,000 | 15,387<br>N=70 | 24,000 |

*Small public = public library serving a population of from 25,000 to 99,999.
**Large public = public library serving a population of over 100,000.

N = number of incumbents

Source: ALA SURVEY OF LIBRARIAN SALARIES, 1984

Table 21. (cont.) Salaries Paid to Beginning Professionals by Type of Library and Region of the U.S. (in dollars)

| Region<br>Type of Library | Southeast | | | West and Southwest | | | All Libraries | | |
|---|---|---|---|---|---|---|---|---|---|
| | Low | Mean | High | Low | Mean | High | Low | Mean | High |
| Small Public* | 9,928 | 13,830<br>N=16 | 23,520 | 12,000 | 17,502<br>N=13 | 26,237 | 9,928 | 15,226<br>N=52 | 26,237 |
| Large Public** | 12,600 | 15,334<br>N=22 | 21,360 | 13,200 | 18,497<br>N=68 | 22,300 | 10,500 | 16,583<br>N=162 | 22,300 |
| 2-year College | 16,000 | 20,494<br>N=5 | 26,472 | 15,000 | 24,612<br>N=4 | 34,250 | 13,500 | 20,439<br>N=15 | 34,250 |
| 4-year College | 13,000 | 16,700<br>N=7 | 22,200 | 14,200 | 17,603<br>N=2 | 21,005 | 9,000 | 18,373<br>N=28 | 33,773 |
| Univ. | 11,016 | 14,625<br>N=16 | 19,640 | 12,000 | 16,605<br>N=27 | 20,464 | 11,016 | 15,699<br>N=60 | 20,464 |
| All | 9,928 | 15,334<br>N=66 | 26,472 | 12,000 | 18,134<br>N=114 | 34,250 | 9,000 | 16,534<br>N=317 | 34,250 |

*Small public = public library serving a population of from 25,000 to 99,999.
**Large public = public library serving a population of over 100,000.

N = number of incumbents

Source: ALA SURVEY OF LIBRARIAN SALARIES, 1984

# 3

## DISCUSSION

### Comments on Results

People interested in a particular type of library or a particular type of work, or a particular region will have their own way of drawing conclusions from the results of this survey. However, the results may be summarized in a very general way by observing mean salaries paid to particular positions, mean salaries paid by particular types of libraries, or mean salaries paid in particular parts of the U.S. With regard to each of these three perspectives, it is possible to look at starting salaries or maximum salaries on the Scheduled Salaries table (Table A for each position) or to look at the Salaries Paid table (Table B).

### Salaries by Position

The thirteen positions are shown in rank order by scheduled starting salary, by scheduled maximum salary, and by salary paid on Tables 22, 23, 24. These three tables could not be combined into a single table because the ranking of the various position titles changes depending on which of these possible salaries is being considered. A similar problem occurs in trying to compare 1984 salaries with 1982 salaries--the rank order is just a little different. To save space and simplify reporting we have used the 1984 ranking but marked with an asterisk positions which were in a different rank order in 1982. Two additional columns are also given: a column showing the dollar amount of change from 1982 to 1984 and a column indicating the percent of change. It is not possible to compare 1982 and 1984 salaries for the three age level positions found mostly in public libraries since the titles and descriptions of those positions was changed on the questionnaire used in 1984. Some observations on those salaries are given later in this section.

Whether one considers scheduled starting salaries, scheduled maximum salaries or salaries paid, the mean reported for all positions increased anywhere from eleven to twenty-three percent from the 1982 survey to the 1984 survey. In the thirty cases where the three types of salary figures could be compared (age level positions excluded) the average increase was fifteen percent. In part this was a result of economic forces influencing all salaries during this period. It is probably also due in part to several changes made in the survey: in 1984 we included ARL libraries which generally have higher salaries than others. Also in 1984 we asked respondents not to report salaries which were at least in part contributed, thus eliminating some low salaries. Finally we prorated nine month and ten month salaries to their twelve month equivalent. This last change was responsible for increases in 137 starting salaries, 133 maximum salaries, and 425 salaries paid.

### Salaries by Type of Library

When one considers salaries by type of library it is useful to separate positions into three groups: the four administrative positions found in all types of libraries (Director, Deputy/Associate Director, Assistant

Director, and Department Head/Branch Head); the six non-administrative positions found in all libraries (Reference/Information Librarian, Cataloger and/or Classifier, Serials Librarian, Audiovisual Librarian, Government Documents Librarian, and Subject Specialist/Bibliographer); and the three positions found primarily in public libraries.

With regard to administrative positions, in both 1982 and 1984 scheduled starting salaries are highest in large public libraries and second highest in universities for Director, Deputy/Associate Director, and Assistant Director. Scheduled maximum salaries in 1984 were highest in universities and second highest in large public libraries except for Assistant Director where the scheduled maximum is highest in 2-year college libraries and second highest in university libraries. Scheduled starting salaries are lowest in 4-year college libraries for all three positions. Scheduled maximums are lowest in 4-year colleges for Director but lowest in small public libraries for the other two positions.

Scheduled starting and maximum salaries for Department Head/Branch Head are highest in 2-year college libraries and second highest in university libraries. For this position both scheduled starting salary and scheduled maximum are lowest in small public libraries.

Salaries paid are highest in large public libraries for Director and Assistant Director and highest in universities for Deputy/Associate Director. For Department Head/Branch Head salaries paid are highest in 2-year colleges and lowest in small public libraries.

With regard to non-administrative positions, both starting and maximum scheduled salaries are highest in 2-year colleges and second highest in universities for Reference Librarian and Cataloger/Classifier. For the other four positions, rankings are mixed with either university, large public or 2-year colleges on top. The scheduled salaries (starting or maximum) are lowest in either small public libraries or 4-year college libraries. Salaries paid are highest in 2-year colleges for four of the six positions and highest in universities for serials librarian and government documents librarian.

Salaries by Region of the U.S.

With regard to the four regions of the U.S. considered for this survey (see Table 25 in Appendix B), salaries are highest for all positions in the West and Southwest regardless of whether one considers means of scheduled starting salaries, scheduled maximum salaries or salaries paid. The only exceptions to this pattern may be seen on tables for Assistant Director and Serials Librarian. Means of scheduled starting salaries are lowest in the Southeast for all positions except Subject Specialist/Bibliographer. Means of the scheduled maximums follow the same pattern. Means of salaries paid are lowest in the Southeast for eleven of the thirteen positions. These findings are not surprising in view of what economists know about regional differences in income for workers of all types. A chart in the Wall Street Journal for

March 4, 1982* shows that incomes have been highest in the Pacific region for twenty years and lowest in the South for the same period. The article points out, however, that these differences are narrowing.

Age Level Positions in Public Libraries

The questionnaire used in the 1982 survey asked for information on salaries scheduled and paid for three positions found only in public libraries:

> Children's and/or Young Adult and/or Adult Services Librarian
> Coordinator, Children's Services
> Coordinator, Adult Services

The positions were combined in this way after consultation with the Executive Directors of the four ALA divisions most concerned: the Association for Library Service to Children (ALSC), the Public Library Association (PLA), the Reference and Adult Services Division (RASD), and the Young Adult Services Division (YASD). After the 1982 report was published, however, several users told us that the data would be more useful if the age level coordinator positions were combined and salaries for children's and/or young adult services librarians were separated from salaries for adult services librarians. Our ALA staff consultants agreed to the suggestion and the questionnaire was changed for the 1984 survey. In 1984 the three positions listed were:

> Children's and/or Young Adult Services Librarian
> Adult Services Librarian
> Coordinator, Adult and/or Young Adult and/or Children's Services

Because of the change, we cannot compare the salaries for any of these positions in 1982 with 1984 salaries. It may be useful to note, however, that on Tables 22, 23 and 24 salaries for the coordinator position are higher than for either services position. In addition, the Adult Services position is always higher than the Children's Services position. In 1982 the two Coordinator positions were always higher than the service positions and the Adult and/or Young Adult Services Coordinator was higher than the Children's Services Coordinator.

---

*Malabre, Alfred L., "Income Differences Between Regions Narrow as a Result of Mobility, More Women at Work," <u>Wall Street Journal</u>, Thursday, March 4, 1982, p. 48.

Table 22. Rank Order of Position Titles by Mean of Scheduled Starting Salaries

| Title | 84 Salary | 82 Salary | Difference Amt | % |
|---|---|---|---|---|
| Director | 26,213 | 22,993 | 3220 | 14 |
| Deputy/Associate Director | 23,096 | 20,539 | 2557 | 12 |
| Assistant Director | 22,235 | 19,269 | 2966 | 15 |
| Coordinator, Adult and/or Young Adult and/or Children's Services | 19,549 | ** | | |
| Subject Specialist/Bibliographer | 18,224 | 15,869 | 2355 | 15 |
| Department Head/Branch Head | 17,991 | 15,928* | 2063 | 13 |
| Government Documents Librarian | 17,915 | 16,148* | 1767 | 11 |
| Audiovisual Librarian | 17,648 | 15,332 | 2316 | 15 |
| Serials Librarian | 17,025 | 14,771 | 2254 | 15 |
| Reference/Information Librarian | 16,595 | 14,498 | 2097 | 14 |
| Cataloger and/or Classifier | 16,416 | 14,647 | 1769 | 12 |
| Adult Services Librarian | 16,606 | ** | | |
| Children's and/or Young Adult Services Librarian | 16,013 | ** | | |

\* = Rank order different in 1982
\*\* = Position not on 1982 questionnaire

SOURCE: ALA SURVEY OF LIBRARIAN SALARIES, 1984

Table 23. Rank Order of Position Titles by Mean of Scheduled Maximum Salaries

| Title | 84 Salary | 82 Salary | Difference Amt | % |
|---|---|---|---|---|
| Director | 37,563 | 32,943 | 4620 | 14 |
| Deputy/Associate Director | 32,253 | 28,237 | 4016 | 14 |
| Assistant Director | 32,026 | 27,833 | 4199 | 13 |
| Subject Specialist/Bibliographer | 27,933 | 23,037 | 4896 | 21 |
| Department Head/Branch Head | 26,616 | 23,262* | 3354 | 14 |
| Serials Librarian | 25,995 | 21,879 | 4116 | 19 |
| Coordinator, Adult and/or Young Adult and/or Children's Services | 25,887 | ** | | |
| Government Documents Librarian | 25,852 | 22,835* | 3017 | 13 |
| Audiovisual Librarian | 25,766 | 22,162* | 3604 | 16 |
| Reference/Information Librarian | 25,102 | 21,428 | 3674 | 17 |
| Cataloger and/or Classifier | 24,539 | 21,528* | 3011 | 14 |
| Adult Services Librarian | 22,856 | ** | | |
| Children's and/or Young Adult Services Librarian | 21,949 | ** | | |

\* = Rank order different in 1982
\*\* = Position not on 1982 questionnaire

SOURCE: ALA SURVEY OF LIBRARIAN SALARIES, 1984

Table 24. Rank Order of Position Titles by Mean of Salaries Paid

| Title | 84 Salary | 82 Salary | Difference Amt | % |
|---|---|---|---|---|
| Director | 32,198 | 27,408 | 4790 | 17 |
| Assistant Director | 29,126 | 23,644 | 5482 | 23 |
| Deputy/Associate Director | 28,691 | 23,637 | 5054 | 21 |
| Coordinator, Adult and/or Young Adult and/or Children's Services | 24,394 | ** | | |
| Subject Specialist/Bibliographer | 23,506 | 19,871 | 3635 | 18 |
| Department Head/Branch Head | 23,259 | 20,080* | 3179 | 16 |
| Government Documents Librarian | 21,228 | 18,634 | 2594 | 14 |
| Reference/Information Librarian | 20,757 | 17,684 | 3073 | 17 |
| Audiovisual Librarian | 20,732 | 18,044* | 2688 | 15 |
| Cataloger and/or Classifier | 20,516 | 17,603 | 2913 | 17 |
| Adult Services Librarian | 19,879 | ** | | |
| Serials Librarian | 19,801 | 16,776 | 3025 | 18 |
| Children's and/or Young Adult Services Librarian | 18,314 | ** | | |

\* = Rank order different in 1982
\*\* = Position not on 1982 questionnaire

SOURCE: ALA SURVEY OF LIBRARIAN SALARIES, 1984

---

Complicating Factors

When designing this survey in 1981 we were aware that several aspects of the patterns of employment in libraries would complicate our efforts. As we talked to people about the 1982 report and considered letters or telephone comments from 1984 respondents, we gained additional insights into several factors which should be taken into consideration when using these results.

The Meaning of "Full-Time"

The questionnaire asked about salaries for full-time positions only, but full-time was not defined. There are at least three problems in this area: How many hours in a week is full-time? How many months in a year is full-time? How do you report people who work full-time in the library but part-time at one job and part-time at another? Although hours per week was not usually noted by respondents, this did happen occasionally, probably because the respondent was unsure if the incumbent should be considered full-time. In such cases, we accepted thirty hours or more per week as full-time. Months in a year was a more difficult problem. In the 1982 survey we asked respondents to indicate the salaries which were for less than twelve months and an Appendix reported how often this happened. Because we were convinced that including these salaries as full-time distorted the means we reported, this procedure was changed in 1984. Respondents were asked to indicate the number of months a salary covered and the computer calculated and recorded twelve months at the same rate. This may be considered a distortion in the direction of inflating the mean but it seemed preferable to what had been done in 1982. Again we show in Appendix E how often less-than-twelve-month salaries occur.

Another complication related to the issue of "full-time" is the fact that one librarian may fill more than one position. For example: a public librarian may work part-time as a children's librarian and part-time as a cataloger; an academic librarian may be a government documents librarian as well as a department head (of government documents department). Survey instructions told the respondent:

> If a staff member works full-time but performs duties of more than one position, list him or her as incumbent in the position which is his or her major responsibility or in the position having the higher salary. List each staff member only once.

The Meaning of "Professional"

As noted earlier, the word "professional" was not defined, but each position was described in such a way that professional responsibility was clearly implied. Instructions told the respondent to list all incumbents in these positions "regardless of academic credentials." We decided to accept the judgment of the respondent that the salaries reported were for professional work but found out, when we called about low salaries (see below), that some respondents had doubts about whether a particular incumbent could be described as "professional." When such doubts were expressed we asked the respondent to make a decision based on the definitions in ALA's statement on "Library Education and Personnel Utilization."

Salaries Below $8,000

When initial printouts of the results of the 1982 survey revealed approximately eighty salaries which seemed very low for full time professional work (i.e. under $9,000), we called twenty of the respondents to ask if a part-time incumbent had been reported by mistake. In several cases that had happened, but in other cases the low salary really was for full-time work. The two categories overlapped, however. The highest part-time salary in these twenty calls was $7,100 and the lowest full-time salary was $6,400. Because it would be very expensive to call all the other libraries reporting low salaries, we established $7,000 as a cut-off point in 1982. All salaries below that amount were assumed to be part-time and were not counted in the results of this survey. We did not repeat the telephone calls in 1984 but did raise the cutoff point to $8,000 (14%). Salaries below $8,000 were dropped on the grounds that they were probably not full-time.

Job Levels or Status

The wording of this questionnaire is based on an assumption that librarians are compensated at a particular amount for doing a particular job (e.g. reference, serials). However, in many libraries that is not true. Some libraries use a system of levels in their compensation structure (e.g. Librarian I, II, III, IV) to account for the background a person brings to a job and the amount of responsibility it entails. Some academic libraries pay salaries based on faculty rank rather than work done. We did not attempt to account for this variety within the structure of our questionnaire.

The strategy was successful in many cases but it caused problems especially in large public libraries and in academic libraries closely tied to a faculty salary structure. Several large public libraries responded that they simply could not take the time to record salaries for each of the many Librarian I's, Librarian II's, and Librarian III's who were scattered among several position titles. Such a library could tell us, for example, that the position title "Reference/Information Librarian" was filled by Librarian I's, Librarian II's, and Librarian III's and therefore had a scheduled salary range which embraced all three, but could not give us the exact salary of each incumbent. Current library records do not facilitate this kind of reporting.

In academic libraries where librarians have faculty rank and titles they are compensated as Instructor, Assistant Professor, Associate Professor or Professor and not as any one of the position titles on our questionnaire. Here again, respondents would tell us that a particular position was filled by persons in one, two, three, or four of these salary ranges and provided corresponding figures. We could create composite ranges as appropriate, but they were very broad ones. Incumbent salaries were a function of the rank, not of the position title.

Employee Benefits

Although the main purpose of this survey was to gain information about salaries, question E was added because we hoped to gather some supplementary information about another aspect of compensation--benefits. We were aware that the matter of employee benefits has many more complexities than could be covered in a single question but hoped that experience with the question could help us to understand employee benefits in the library community. The data in Table 20 is rough for several reasons. For one thing, a good number of respondents were unable to give us the figure because the library itself did not keep the records necessary to calculate it. Others were puzzled because the questionnaire did not provide a definition of "employee benefits" and others were confused by the instruction for calculating total employee benefits as a percent of total payroll. This was especially bothersome to academic respondents whose payroll included substantial payments to students who worked part-time and did not receive benefits.

Because most of the phone calls made to clear up confusion on responses to the 1982 survey were made with regard to the question on benefits, we considered dropping it from the 1984 questionnaire. Readers of the report claimed it was useful, however, and the question was repeated in the 1984 survey. Once again, this question necessitated the largest number of phone calls to respondents.

Appendix A

## COMPENSATION AND EMPLOYEE BENEFITS

1. Employee Benefits: Basic Concepts and Current Issues
2. Salary Surveys Providing Information on Library Workers
3. ALA Policies Relating to Salary Issues
4. Selected Bibliography on Compensation and Employee Benefits

Appendix A-1

Employee Benefits: Basic Concepts and Current Issues

by Jeniece Guy
Assistant Director, ALA Office for Library Personnel Resources

History and Background of Employee Benefits Programs

Insurance programs for employees were established by some companies as early as the 1900s; however, in the years prior to World War II the average employee's compensation was entirely cash, the wages or salaries paid. In the 1930s the federal government instituted a variety of social insurance programs but benefits provided by employers in the form of non-cash compensation did not become widespread until World War II. The wage ceiling imposed by the federal government during World War II caused businesses to expand their benefit packages in place of wage increases to attract new workers and to retain current workers. Employee benefits were once called fringe benefits because they accounted for only a small portion of an employee's total compensation. Today benefits account for 37-40 percent of payroll[1] and most people in the personnel field no longer use the term fringe benefits.

Employee benefits can be divided into the following categories:

1. Those required by statute (i.e., social security; unemployment compensation and worker's compensation).

2. Security and welfare (e.g., pension, health insurance, dental insurance, disability, etc).

3. Employee services (e.g., discount purchase plans, tuition aid, credit unions and recreational programs).

4. Pay for time not worked (e.g., vacation, holiday, sick time, etc.).

5. Extra compensation (e.g., profit sharing, savings plans, etc.). [2]

Employee benefits have experienced dramatic growth in the past ten years. In 1953 benefits in business and industry accounted for 19.2 percent of payroll, in 1963, 25.6 percent, and 32.7 percent in 1973.[3] The rate of growth averages out to ten percent per year. There are three major reasons for the growth of benefit programs over the past twenty years. First, unions and employees have demanded new and increased benefits. As a new benefit begins to be publicized, it is viewed as a standard. A prime example of this is dental insurance which was uncommon in 1973 and is a standard benefit today. Government action has regulated many aspects of the employee benefit program and has certainly contributed to increased costs. Finally, inflation has affected the cost of these programs.

The aspect of benefits which grew the fastest between 1963 and 1973 was pay for time not worked. The number of paid holidays increased and many companies decreased the years of service required in order to earn longer vacations or added new types of leave such as personal days and leaves for death in the family.[4] The fastest growing type of benefit cost between 1973 and 1983 was health insurance. The runaway rise in health insurance was in part due to inflation and in part due to the development of new and costly health care technology.

One factor which has influenced benefit plans and costs is legislation and other government action. Below is a summary of the most influential legislation and court decisions between 1973 and 1983.

The Employee Retirement Income Security Act (ERISA) regulates pension benefit plans and welfare benefit plans. ERISA mandates certain eligibility requirements and also dictates when a pension must be vested. The employer has three different choices but the most frequently chosen by employers is 100 percent vesting after ten years. Vesting is the point at which the money in an employee's plan legally belongs to the employee.

In 1978, the Supreme Court's decision in City of Los Angeles, Department of Water and Power et al vs. Manhart et al (435 U.S. 702, 17 FEP Cases 395) made it illegal to make unequal contributions to pension plans based on sex.

In 1978, Congress amended the 1967 Age Discrimination in Employment Act. Prior to 1978, the act had made it illegal to discriminate against employees in the 40-64 age bracket. The 1978 amendments extended protection to employees age 65-70. Mandatory retirement prior to age 70 became illegal.

The Pregnancy Discrimination Act of 1978 amended the 1964 Civil Rights Act, requiring employers to treat pregnant female employees in the same manner they treat other employees with a temporary disability. The law covers sick leave, disability, health and medical insurance.

The final piece of legislation which has affected benefit programs is the Health Maintenance Organization Act of 1973. This law requires employees who furnish traditional health and medical insurance plans to employers to also provide a health maintenance organization plan. Health Maintenance Organizations (HMOs) are prepaid health plans in which almost all medical expenses, including routine physicals, are covered. The employees must use the HMO's facilities in order to avail themselves of the coverage. The great advantage an HMO has over conventional health plans is that routine and preventive medical care is covered. The major disadvantage of an HMO has always been that individuals do not have a choice of doctor. Recently, however, HMOs have begun to structure their services so that the patient chooses a primary care physician.

## Objectives of an Employee Benefits Program

Employee benefits were originally implemented to help organizations recruit and retain employees and this remains the rationale for offeringbenefit packages. How can organizations ensure that the benefit package fulfills this objective? William Holley and Kenneth Jennings suggest three procedures designed to link the benefits package with organizational objectives: determining appropriate benefits, communicating benefit programs to employees and monitoring benefit plans to determine their cost effectiveness.[5]

In the past personnel managers who sought to determine appropriate benefits have relied primarily on a demographic analysis of their employees. The personnel manager would analyze such factors as the average age of employees, marital status and sex. It is assumed that younger employees want more time off; employees with families are interested in health and other insurance coverage; and older employees are concerned with savings plans--either for their children's college expenses or for retirement.[6] While these generalizations may hold true, today's employees often do not fit a specific pattern. A more precise way of determining appropriate benefits is to survey the employees to determine how various benefits are perceived.

Results of a survey of a benefits program will:

.show the relative importance of specific benefits to employees

.identify the benefits that need improvement

.identify new benefits employees would like

.show whether employees would prefer a change in the proportions of direct compensation and benefits.[7]

While a survey can be a useful technique and employers can learn much from it, it can raise employee expectations that new benefits will be created or benefit packages will be improved.

## Current Issues

Cost effectiveness or cost control has become one of the biggest issues in benefits administration today. The dramatic increase in the percentage of payroll occupied by benefits is one reason why cost control is an issue. The biggest culprit in the rising cost of benefits has been the health and medical insurance. Health care costs have increased 94 percent between 1973 and 1980.[8] Companies are undertaking various programs to reduce health care costs. Some companies are doing such things as paying for physical exams or providing free blood pressure screening. Other programs are designed to have a preventive effect through exercise and recreational programs, stress management classes, counseling on diet and nutrition, and stop smoking clinics.

While an emphasis on preventive medicine can help reduce the costs of health insurance by reducing the number of claims, many companies have found it necessary to make actual cuts in benefits. Several companies have taken such cost cutting measures as increasing the amount of the deductible, requiring mandatory second opinions for elective surgery and other optional treatment, pre-admission testing on an outpatient basis, and using an audit firm. Other companies are bypassing insurance companies altogether and reimbursing doctors and hospitals directly. In the private sector, health insurance, as well as other benefits, have traditionally been paid entirely by the employee; however, a few companies have been introducing contributory (employee pays a share of the insurance costs) health insurance packages. Two benefits experts believe that the majority of medical plans will remain non-contributory but more employers will require that the employees share the costs of family coverage.[9]

Perhaps the most popular way to contain benefit plan costs is the flexible or cafeteria benefits approach in which employees are allowed some flexibility in selecting their benefits. There are three variations of the flexible benefit plan. The first, called a core plan, provides employees with a basic core benefit package (e.g., life insurance, disability, vacation and health insurance). Employees are then given a benefits allowance over and above the basic core package. They "spend" this allowance as they choose. One employee might "spend" his or her credits to purchase additional life insurance while another might purchase dental insurance.

An alternative is to let employees retain the same coverage they had prior to the introduction of the flexible plan or allow them to choose lower core benefits and apply the "credits" toward some other benefit. For example, an employee may elect a higher health insurance deductible or less vacation and apply that "credit" toward a company sponsored day care or dental plan.

Another example of flexible benefits is alternate sets of packages, each designed to appeal to a different demographic group of employees. The packages, each designed to be of equal value, are targeted to employee groups such as those employees with a non-working spouse and children, single employees, single parents, or dual career couples. The employee selects the total package best suited to his or her needs but cannot vary specific components of the package. Although this type of plan offers the employee less flexibility, it is much easier to administer.

The major advantages of a flexible benefits plan are:

.improved job satisfaction and morale

.cost containment/cost effectiveness

.a way of introducing new benefits at a minimum cost to the employer

.increased employee awareness of the costs of benefits

Disadvantages include:

- high initial cost of implementing a flexible benefit plan

- difficulty in administering, except in the targeted package programs

- uncertainty of the tax status of some aspects of flexible benefits programs.

Employee Benefits in Business and Libraries

What types of benefits are most popular in business? In a survey of non-statutory benefits conducted by the Chamber of Commerce and reported by Nation's Business, the most commonly provided are life, hospital, surgical and major medical insurance and paid vacations. The insurance plans were offered by 100 percent of employers and 95 percent offered paid vacations. Ninety-five percent also offered paid holidays. Eighty-six percent provided private pension plans. Seventy-eight percent of the companies surveyed offered paid sick leave. Forty-nine percent offered long term disability plans, and 45 percent offered non-production bonuses such as Christmas bonuses, service and suggestion awards. Twenty percent offered savings plans with the employer making a contribution to the savings plan. Thirty-five percent of the companies offered dental plans. Twenty-eight percent had tuition reimbursement plans. Seventeen percent provided discounts on company products and services.[10]

How do these benefits compare with the benefits provided by libraries? Surveys of the benefits in libraries have not been plentiful; however, there are a few sources of information. Personnel Policies in Libraries by Nancy Patton Van Zant gives some information as to the type of benefits provided in libraries. The survey conducted by Van Zant included academic and public libraries and the information is reported out in five categories: public libraries serving a population of less than 20,000; public libraries serving 20,000 to 99,999; public libraries serving 1,000,000 and up; four-year college libraries; and university libraries. The Van Zant survey included only nine of the benefits listed in the Chamber of Commerce survey.

The most prevalent benefits in libraries are sick leave (98 percent report paid sick leave), paid vacation (98 percent) and paid holidays (98 percent). This is in contrast to private business where the most prevalent benefits are life and health insurance and paid vacations. Although the percentage is not as high as in business, most libraries (95 percent) provide health insurance. A smaller number (79 percent) provided life insurance. Libraries did better than businesses in one other benefit area besides sick leave--96 percent provided a private pension plan as opposed to 86 percent of businesses.[11] Van Zant did note that some libraries mentioned dental plans or tuition reimbursement even though these were not included in the questionnaire.

Although this comparison will give a rough idea of the differences between benefits in libraries and businesses, there is no way to provide a more in-depth comparison of the level of benefits—for example, the dollar amount of health and life insurance. The Van Zant survey also does not indicate whether the benefit plans are contributory or whether the library pays the full amount of coverage. In business, the employer typically pays for the entire amount of insurance and pension plan coverage.

Another way to determine the level of benefits is to look at the percentage of payroll that is spent on benefits. As cited earlier, businesses typically spend 37-40 percent of payroll.

The ALA Survey of Librarian Salaries shows an average of 19 percent for all types of libraries (Table 20). This figure varies slightly by geographic region. The Southeast has the lowest average of 16.9 percent. The figure also varies somewhat by type of library. The figure is highest in large public libraries and two year colleges (20 percent) and lowest in four year colleges (15.8 percent). Libraries, of course, usually provide the benefits offered by the parent institution so the library administrator often may not have much to say about the level or type of benefits the library offers.

Library directors and other library managers may not always have as much direct input into the design of benefit packages that managers in business and industry do; however, library administrators will need to remain aware of issues and trends in benefits administration. The cost benefit packages in libraries will continue to grow and benefits will be an important part of library personnel management.

NOTES

[1] Fred D. Lindsey, "Employee Benefits, Then and Now," Nation's Business 68 (no. 8 August, 1981), 63.

[2] Colman S. Ives, "Benefits and Services," in ASPA Handbook of Personnel and Industrial Relations, ed. by Dale Yoder and Herbert G. Henneman, Jr., 2 (Washington: Bureau of National Affairs, 1975), 6-186.

[3] Ibid. p. 6-187.

[4] Ibid.

[5] William Holley and Kenneth Jennings, Personnel Management: Functions and Issues (Chicago: Dryden Press, 1983), 389.

[6] Ibid. p. 391.

[7] Ibid. p. 390.

[8] Margaret A. Benston and Jay R. Schuster, "Executive Compensation and Employee Benefits," in Human Resources Management in the 1980's, ed. by Stephen J. Carroll and Randall S. Schuler (Washington: Bureau of National Affairs, 1983), 6-17.

[9] Ibid. p. 6-30.

[10] Fred D. Lindsey, "Employee Benefits," pp. 62, 63, 65.

[11] Nancy Patton Van Zant, ed., Personnel Policies in Libraries (New York: Neal-Schuman, 1980), xxv.

Appendix A-2

## Salary Surveys Providing Information on Library Workers

by Margaret Myers
Director, ALA Office for Library Personnel Resources

The library salary surveys listed below are primarily conducted on a regular schedule (annual or biennial) and on a regional or national basis. The library literature should be monitored for reports of one-time surveys by individual libraries or associations. Some state library agencies collect salary and benefits data as part of their ongoing statistical gathering efforts from libraries within their own state. There is wide variation, however, in what data are collected and how these are compiled and reported. Most collect only public library data. Academic and school library data may be collected by other state agencies. In addition, some state library associations collect salary data, issue recommended salary guidelines, set minimum salaries for professional positions, or publish reports in association journals or newsletters. A list of state library agencies and association addresses can be found in The Bowker Annual of Library and Book Trade Information.

Individual libraries will sometimes conduct private surveys of institutions of comparable size or in the same geographical area, either through an outside consulting firm or by calling libraries informally. For the most part, these surveys are not published, although the initiating library will often share results with participating libraries. Some librarians are also conducting surveys which compare their salaries with other professions and occupations within their jurisdiction in an effort to achieve pay equity with positions requiring comparable skills, effort, responsibilities and working conditions.

For guidance in using salary surveys in a compensation program, readers may wish to consult "Employee Compensation and the Library Manager" by Jeniece Guy in the 1982 ALA Survey of Librarian Salaries.

ACADEMIC LIBRARIES

Association of Research Libraries. ARL Annual Salary Survey. Washington, D.C.: ARL.

The annual survey shows median and beginning professional salaries for positions in all ARL libraries. In addition, tables present the average salaries for nineteen position categories and display findings on the present incumbents of these positions by sex and minority group membership, and by geographical location, size, and type of institution.

Order from: ARL, 1527 New Hampshire Ave., N.W., Washington, DC 20036. The 1983 survey is available for $8/ARL members or $10/nonmembers.

College and University Personnel Association. Administrative Compensation
Survey Report. Washington, D.C.: CUPA.

Annual survey collects data on ninety-four college and university administrative positions by type and size of institution. Directors of library services and deans of library and information science programs are included. A summary report of median salaries from the above survey is usually reported in the Chronicle of Higher Education (1983-84 survey summary is in February 22, 1984 issue.)

College and University Personnel Association. Faculty Salary Survey by
Discipline and Rank in State Colleges and Universities. Washington,
D.C.: CUPA.

College and University Personnel Association. Faculty Salary Survey by
Discipline and Rank in Private Colleges and Universities.
Washington, D.C.: CUPA.

Annual surveys collect data for five faculty ranks in 41 disciplines and major fields. Communications, Communication Technologies, Computer and Information Sciences, and Library and Archival Sciences are included. A summary report of median salaries is usually published in the Chronicle of Higher Education (1983-84 survey summary is in February 29, 1984 issue).

The surveys are available from CUPA, 11 Dupont Circle, Suite 120, Washington, DC 20036; Ad Comp is $25 for association members and $150 to nonmembers; Faculty Salary Surveys are each $10 to members and $20 to nonmembers.


PUBLIC LIBRARIES


Allen County Public Library. Statistics of Public Libraries in the United
States and Canada Serving 100,000 Population or More. Fort Wayne,
Ind.: Allen County Public Library.

Biennial report since 1958 gives salaries for director, assistant director, and beginning professional positions in large public libraries. The 1983 report, however, did not include assistant director salaries.

Latest report published in June, 1983 is available from Allen County Public Library, 900 Webster St., P.O. Box 2270, Ft. Wayne, IN 46801 for $5.00 in hard copy or $40 for machine-readable forms (five mini-diskettes for use on an Apple computer with Visicalc Expand).

An article by Rick J. Ashton and Steven Fortriede based on the salary data from the report is scheduled to appear in a forthcoming issue of Library Journal. The data are analyzed to show relationships between the sex of the director, geographic area, population served, per capital support, and beginning librarian salaries.

International City Management Association. "Salaries of Municipal Officials" in Municipal Year Book. Washington, D.C.: ICMA.

Chief librarian salaries for public libraries are included with earnings of other city department heads. These are reported by geographic region, population size, city type (i.e., central, suburban, independent) and form of government. The mean, median, and first and third quartiles are included for libraries serving ten different population groups ranging from under 2,500 to over 1,000,000.

The Municipal Year Book is usually published in April or May of each year and includes salary data for previous year. This information is also reported in a March or April issue of the Baseline Data Report. Compensation, a new publication on salaries and fringe benefits of municipal officials, is published annually. For details, contact ICMA, 1120 G Street, NW, Washington, DC 20005.

Memphis-Shelby County Public Library and Information Center. Statistics of Southern Public Libraries. Memphis, Tenn.

Annual survey of libraries with budgets of $300,000 or more in the southeastern and southwestern states gives salary information for individual libraries for chief librarian, assistant librarian, department head, beginning professional and two support staff positions.

Public Library Quarterly will publish this survey on an annual basis. Vol. 4 (4), winter 1983 contains the 1983 survey. The 1984 survey is scheduled for the winter 1984 issue.

Metropolitan Washington Library Council. Annual Statistical Data for Public Libraries in Metropolitan Washington. Washington, D.C.: Metropolitan Washington Council of Governments.

Annual survey of nine public libraries in Virginia, Maryland, and District of Columbia includes salary ranges for clerical, subprofessional, professional, associate director, and director positions and employee benefits information. Usually published in March for previous fiscal year.

Fiscal Year 1983 report is available for $5.00 to nonmembers and free to members from Metropolitan Washington Library Council, 1875 I St. N.W., Washington, D.C. 20006.

Sandstedt, Carl R. <u>Salary Survey: West-North-Central States</u>. St. Peters, Mo.: St. Charles City-County Library.

Annual survey provides data for directors, assistant directors, department heads, starting MLS, and several support positions for public libraries, systems, and state agencies in West-North-Central States (North Dakota, South Dakota, Nebraska, Kansas, Minnesota, Iowa, Missouri). Average salaries are presented by size of library budget.

Usually available in April for previous calendar year. Send stamped, self-addressed envelope to Carl Sandstedt, Director, St. Charles City-County Library, 425 Spencer Rd., Box 529, St. Peters, MO 63376.

SCHOOL LIBRARIES

Educational Research Service, Inc. <u>National Survey of Salaries and Wages in Public Schools</u>. Arlington, Va.: ERS.

Since 1974-75, ERS has published an annual report of salaries for public school personnel, which includes data for school librarians and library clerks. Usually published in three volumes, the report covers scheduled salaries for professional personnel and actual salaries paid for professional and support personnel by enrollment group, per pupil expenditure, and geographic region.

The 1983-84 report, published in 1984, costs $28 for each of the three volumes; available from ERS, 1800 N. Kent St., Arlington, VA 22209.

Miller, Marilyn L., and Moran, Barbara B. "Expenditures for Resources in School Library Media Centers, FY '82-'83." <u>School Library Journal</u> 30 (October, 1983), 105-114.

As part of a report on budgets for and expenditures by school library media centers, some median and mean salary data for media specialists are reported by level of school, region, size of population served by school district and number of students. Included are comparisons of private and public schools and schools with and without district level library media coordinators. <u>SLJ</u> projects an annual series of similar reports.

National Education Association. <u>Estimates of School Statistics</u>. Washington, D.C.: NEA.

Annual statistical data for the 50 states and District of Columbia includes estimated average annual salaries of total instructional staff and of classroom teachers by state and region. Librarian data are not given separately, however, but grouped with teachers, principals, supervisors, guidance and psychological personnel and related instructional workers.

The annual compilation is usually available in February. Education Week, March 23, 1983, p. 15 included a summary of the 1982-83 data. The 1983-84 report was published in 1984. For price information, contact NEA Distribution Center, The Academic Building, Saw Mill Rd., West Haven, CT 06516.

SPECIAL LIBRARIES

American Association of Law Libraries. "Statistical Survey of Law School Libraries and Librarians." Chicago: AALL.

Annual survey based on joint questionnaire by AALL, American Bar Association and Association of American Law Schools. Includes median salaries and benefits of head law school librarians and full time professional law librarians in the U.S. by size of library. The 1981 survey is in the Law Library Journal 75 (Fall, 1982), p. 540+. The 1982 and 1983 surveys will be in v. 76 no. 3, Summer 1983 which will reach subscribers in late 1984. Computer printouts are also available. Contact David A. Thomas, AALL Statistics Coordinator, Law Library, Brigham Young University, Provo, UT 84602.

In the past, periodic salary surveys of county, state and private law librarians have been included in the Law Library Journal. There are no immediate plans for new surveys at this time.

Association of Academic Health Sciences Library Directors and Houston Academy of Medicine-Texas Medical Center Library. Annual Statistics of Medical School Libraries in the United States and Canada. Houston, Texas.

Salaries are provided for director, associate director, division head, department head, other librarians, and entry level positions. Minimum, maximum and mean are provided for the positions and arranged by region.

Edited by Richard Lyders, the 1982-83 report published in 1983 is the sixth edition of this survey. Available from Houston Academy of Medicine-Texas Medical Center Library, Jesse H. Jones Library Building, Houston, TX 77030; $40 for members, $65 for nonmembers.

Medical Library Association. "MLA Salary Survey." Chicago: MLA.

A salary survey of Medical Library Association members was summarized in the MLA News, No. 155/May 1983 ("Salary Survey Results," pp. 1, 7-10). Data are provided by geographic area, type of institution, primary area of responsibility, sex, race/ethnic group.

The full report will be available in the summer of 1984 from MLA, Suite 3208, 919 N. Michigan Ave., Chicago, IL 60611; price to be determined. At this time, MLA does not have plans to repeat the survey.

Special Libraries Association. "SLA Salary Survey." <u>Special Libraries</u>. New York: SLA.

Since 1967, SLA has conducted an in-depth salary survey of members every three years and reported the results in <u>Special Libraries</u>, with the exception of the latest (1982) survey issued as a separate publication. Salaries are reported at the 25th, 50th (median) and 75th percentiles and contain breakdowns by industry, geographic region, administrative responsibility, sex, education level, experience. Annual updates, using only 25 percent of the membership and a shortened form, were started in 1977 and are used in years between the triennial surveys.

The 1982 Salary Survey was published in 1983 as the <u>SLA Triennial Salary Survey</u> and is available for $20 from SLA, 235 Park Ave. S., New York, NY 10003. A summary was issued as the "1983 Salary Survey Update" in <u>Special Libraries</u> 74 (October 1983), 386-387. The October 1984 issue of <u>Special Libraries</u> will report on the 1984 Salary Survey Update. A 1985 triennial in-depth survey will follow.


STATE LIBRARY AGENCIES


American Library Association. Association of Specialized and Cooperative Library Agencies. "Salary Data-State Library Agencies." Chicago: ALA.

Annual survey provides information on the minimum and maximum salary for each state for a variety of positions: state librarian, assistant director, director of reference or reader services, coordinator of LSCA/ESEA titles, senior supervisors or chief consultants, consultants, specialists, and beginning professionals.

Usually available by the end of each year. For copy, send self-addressed, stamped envelope to ASCLA/ALA, 50 E. Huron, Chicago, IL 60611. The survey is also published every other year as an appendix in <u>The State Library Agencies: A Survey Project Report</u>, published by ASCLA. The 1982 salary survey was published in the sixth edition of the report in 1983.


OTHER


Altman, Ellen, and Pratt, Allan. <u>Library Compensation Review: A Quarterly Survey of Salaries and Benefits Offered by Employers of Librarians and Information Specialists</u>. Tucson, Ariz.: University of Arizona Graduate Library School, v. 1 - winter 1982 - .

Although not a direct survey of library salaries, this quarterly periodical tabulates and summarizes salary and other information contained in job advertisements in ten periodicals and other announcements during the previous quarter.

Available by subscription for $25/year from: Graduate Library School, College of Education, University of Arizona, Attn: LCR-F, Tucson, AZ 85721.

Association for Library and Information Science Education. Library and
    Information Science Education Statistical Report.
State College, Pa.: ALISE, 1980-.

Average and median salaries for faculty and administrators in ALISE member schools are provided in this annual report by sex, rank and term of appointment.

All four editions of the report are available from ALISE, 471 Park Lane, State College, PA 16803 for $25 each. Annual report usually published in the summer.

International Personnel Management Association. Pay Rates in the Public
    Sector. Washington, D.C.: IPMA.

Annual survey of 62 selected jobs in federal, state, county and municipal government with minimum, maximum and average salaries for various geographical regions and types of government. Beginning-level librarians and librarians at the second level of responsibility are the only two library positions analyzed.

Full report available from IPMA, 1850 K St. NW, Suite 870, Washington, DC 20006; $10 for members; $25 nonmembers.

Learmont, Carol, and Van Houton, Stephen. "Placements and Salaries 1982:
    Slowing Down", Library Journal 108 (September 15, 1983), 1760-1766.

Annual survey since 1951 of recent graduates of ALA-accredited library education programs (usually published in a late summer or fall issue of Library Journal with data from previous calendar year.) For each reporting school, the low, high, average and median salaries are reported for men, women, and total placements. This information is also provided for five regions of the U.S. and Canada. Additional tables show the distribution of high and low salaries by type of library for men and women, the effect of experience on beginning salaries, and comparison of salaries by type of library.

EMPLOYEE BENEFITS

Although some states collect data on employee benefits, little information is collected on a regional or national level on a regular basis. The Orlando (Florida) Public Library "Summary of Work Benefits Survey" which surveyed large public libraries on an annual basis will no longer be published by Orlando. The Public Library Quarterly hopes to publish information on benefits packages on a regular basis starting with the fall 1984 issue. A more detailed report will also be available for sale. For further information, contact Dick Waters, Dallas Public Library, 1515 Young St., Dallas, TX 75201.

SALARY SURVEYS FOR OTHER LIBRARY WORKERS

For salary data on support staff or professional/specialist positions other than librarians, the following surveys are suggested as a start.

U.S. Department of Labor, Bureau of Labor Statistics Area Wage Surveys. Each year surveys are done in over eighty standard metropolitan areas. The surveys concentrate on clerical and manual labor occupations; however, these will be useful as a source of pay data for clerical positions.

The Bureau also publishes Professional, Administrative, Technical and Clerical Surveys. Primary fields covered are accounting, law, personnel management, engineering, chemistry, retail, clerical supervisory, drafting and clerical. Once again these surveys may provide useful data on non-librarian professional or specialist positions and on clerical positions.

The Administrative Management Society, Maryland Road, Willow Grove, PA 19090 also conducts a survey of clerical, data processing and middle management jobs.

Data on salaries for two professional specializations often found in libraries, personnel specialist and information processing specialist, can be obtained from associations in their respective fields. These are:

American Federation of Information Processing Societies, 1815 N. Lynn St., Suite 800, Arlington, VA 22209 conducts a salary survey for information processing positions.

American Society for Personnel Administration, 606 N. Washington Street, Alexandria, VA 22314 conducts an annual salary survey of personnel and industrial relations professionals.

Sources of information about salary surveys in general can be found in Available Pay Survey Reports: An Annotated Bibliography (2d ed.) by Steven Langer (1980). (Available in three volumes from Abbott, Langer and Associates, P.O. Box 275, Park Forest, IL 60466.)

Appendix A-3

## ALA Policies Relating To Salary Issues

The following are policies endorsed by the ALA Council and included in the "ALA Policy Manual" which appears annually in the ALA Handbook of Organization.

Policy #54.3  Comparable Rewards

The American Library Association supports salary administration which gives reasonable and comparable recognition to positions having administrative, technical, subject, and linguistic requirements. It is recognized that all such specialist competencies can be intellectually vigorous and meet demanding professional operational needs. In administering such a policy, it can be a useful guide that, in major libraries, as many nonadministrative specialities be assigned to the top classifications as are administrative staff. Whenever possible there should be as many at the top rank with less than 30 percent administrative load as there are at the highest rank carrying over 70 percent administrative load.

Policy #54.8  The Library's Pay Plan

Libraries should have a well-constructed and well-administered pay plan based on systematic analysis and evaluation of jobs in the library and which will assure equal pay for equal work. (Note: For text of full statement, see following page.)

Policy #54.9  Permanent Part-Time Employment

The right to earn a living includes a right to part-time employment on a par with full-time employment, including prorated pay and fringe benefits, opportunity for advancement and protection of tenure, access to middle and upper level jobs, and exercise of full responsibilities at any level.

ALA shall create more voluntarily chosen upgraded permanent part-time jobs in its own organization and supports similar action on the part of all libraries.

Policy #54.10  Equal Opportunity and Salaries

The American Library Association supports and works for the achievement of equal salaries and opportunity for employment and promotion for men and women.

The Association fully supports the concept of comparable wages for comparable work that aims at levels of pay for female-oriented occupations equal to those of male-oriented occupations; ALA therefore supports all legal and legislative efforts to achieve wages for library workers commensurate with wages in other occupations with similar qualifications, training, and responsibilities.

ALA particularly supports the efforts of those library workers who have documented, and are legally challenging, the practice of discriminatory salaries, and whose success will benefit all library workers throughout the nation.

Policy #54.18  <u>Advertising Salary Ranges</u>

ALA and its units establish as policy the practice of listing in all ALA publications the salary ranges established for open positions and the policy that salary ranges be given for positions listed in any placement services provided by ALA and its units.

<u>Full Text of Policy # 54.8:  The Library's Pay Plan*</u>

The American Library Association believes that an important factor in establishing and maintaining good library service is adequate pay for library employees as exemplified in a well-constructed and well-administered pay plan. A knowledge of the principles on which sound salary administration is based must be the foundation of an equitable pay plan. To aid the library's governing board, its administration, and its staff in the formulation, promulgation, and operation of such a pay plan, the ALA Board on Personnel Administration sets forth in a series of related statements the principles of salary planning and administration.

1. A sound pay plan will be predicated on a systematic analysis and evaluation of jobs in the library, and will reflect the current organization and objectives of the library, recognizing different levels of difficulty and responsibility inherent in various positions, whether these are classifed as professional, nonprofessional, administrative, specialist, maintenance, or trade; the relationship among positions in terms of difficulty and responsibility will thus be expressed in a unified plan which will integrate all types of service and will assure equal pay for equal work.

---

*Note:  This policy was passed by the ALA Council in July 1955. It still remains a useful statement regarding the administration of a library's pay plan. Readers should note, however, that the references to the Board on Personnel Administration are not applicable since this unit is no longer in existence.

2. An equitable salary schedule will be provided for each class of position which is comparable to that received by persons employed in analogous work in the area and required to have analogous training and qualifications.

   The salaries of nonprofessional employees, maintenance and skilled trade workers employed by the library system will compare with those of local workers performing similar duties. The salary schedules for professional library positions, in the case of the community where the pay scale does not meet competing rates outside, may need to exceed the prevailing local level for other professional personnel. Since the recruiting of professionally trained librarians is on a nation-wide basis, the library system must compete with rates paid in the country as a whole in order to obtain and retain a high quality of professional personnel. In libraries in educational institutions (elementary, secondary, and higher education) the professional librarians will normally be on the faculty pay plan, with the salary schedules of the various classes of faculty rank adjusted to compensate equitably for such factors as shorter vacations and longer work week; where a separate pay plan is used, it will be comparable with that of the faculty and adjusted to compensate equitably for such factors as vacation and work week.

3. An equitable salary schedule will provide for each class of position a minimum and a maximum salary and a series of increments within each salary range, such increments to be granted on the basis of demonstrated competence, individual development (whether through growth on the job or through formal education), and attitude.

4. The library system in developing a pay plan, and in reviewing it to maintain its adequacy, will identify one or more key positions in the professional and in the other services, set salary schedules for these positions which are comparable to prevailing rates for such positions, and develop and adjust the salary schedule for other levels of positions in relation to the salary schedules set for each of these key positions.

5. The pay plan ladder consisting of the salary schedules for the various classes of positions will provide an orderly progression from the lowest to the highest schedule, with each schedule reflecting properly the difference in level of duties and responsibilities of positions in that classification from those in the schedule below and above it but without wide gaps or serious overlapping between schedules.

6. An equitable pay plan will reflect living costs in the community, the cost of maintaining an appropriate level of living, and the ability of the jurisdiction to pay for the service.

7. All policies and rules concerning the operation and administration of the pay plan will be set forth clearly in writing and will accompany the pay plan.

8. Though final approval and adoption of the pay plan and rules for its operation rest with the governing board and administration of the library, it is desirable that the library staff participates in the formulation of both the plan and its operating rules.

9. Each staff member will be informed of the salary schedule for his or her class of position, of the relation of that schedule to the pay plan as a whole, and of the policies and rules governing the operation of the plan.

The current studies of the ALA Board on Personnel Administration giving salary data for key positions will provide useful material for the library system in developing and maintaining the adequacy of its pay plan.

Appendix A-4

## Selected Bibliography on Compensation and Employee Benefits

Note: The 1982 <u>ALA Survey of Librarian Salaries</u> contained a selected bibliography on compensation which readers may wish to consult since many of these references are still useful. Items listed below have been published since that previous listing was compiled.

Bartley, Douglas L. <u>Job Evaluation; Wage and Salary Administration</u>. Reading, Mass.: Addison-Wesley, 1981.

Brennan, E. James. "Everything You Need to Know About Salary Ranges." <u>Personnel Journal</u> 63 (March, 1983), 10-16.

Britton, Donald E. "Rational Salary Management." <u>Personnel Journal</u> 62 (October, 1983), 832-835.

Carter, Michael F., and Shapiro, Kenneth P. "Develop a Proactive Approach to Benefits Planning." <u>Personnel Journal</u> 62 (July, 1983), 562-566.

Ellig, Bruce R. "What's Ahead in Compensation and Benefits." <u>Management Review</u> 72 (August, 1983), 56-61.

Fielder, Barbara L. "Conducting a Wage and Salary Survey." <u>Personnel Journal</u> 61 (December, 1982), 879-880.

Freedman, Sara M.; Montanari, John R.; and Keller, Robert T. "The Compensation Program: Balancing Organizational and Employee Needs." <u>Compensation Review</u> 14 (Second Quarter, 1982), 47-53.

Greene, Robert J., and Roberts, Russell G. "Strategic Integration of Compensation and Benefits." <u>Personnel Administrator</u> 28 (May, 1983), 79-80+.

<u>Handbook of Wage and Salary Administration</u>, edited by Milton L. Rock. 2nd ed. New York: McGraw-Hill, 1984.

Houriham, Thomas W. "Help Employees Understand Their Benefits." <u>Personnel Administrator</u> 28 (April, 1983), 92 +.

McCaffery, Robert M. <u>Managing the Employee Benefits Program</u>. Rev. ed. New York: AMACOM, 1983.

McMillan, John D., and Williams, Valerie C. "The Elements of Effective Salary Administration Program." <u>Personnel Journal</u> 61 (November, 1982), 832-838.

"Pro and Con: Merit Pay." <u>Personnel Administrator</u> 28 (October, 1983), 60-63 +.

Wallace, Marc J., Jr., and Fay, Charles H. <u>Compensation Theory and Practice</u>. Boston: Kent, 1983.

Appendix B

TECHNICAL CONSIDERATIONS

Formation of Library Groups

The survey universe included two types of libraries--public and academic. Public libraries serving populations of less than 25,000 were excluded. Although we realized that this would eliminate a large number of public libraries, we also knew that many of those excluded employ only a few professional librarians on a full time basis.* Since we were seeking information about thirteen specific positions, it did not make sense to incur the costs involved in sampling small libraries. We separated the remaining public libraries into two classes--those serving populations of from 25,000 to 99,999 and those serving populations of over 100,000.

The academic library universe was stratified into three classes:

Library in a 2-year college (offers at least two but less than four years)
Library in a 4-year college (offers four or five year baccalaurelate or four years undergraduate work but not conferring bachelor's degree)
Library in college or university offering work beyond bachelor's level.

This stratification was based on the "Highest Level of Offering" categories used by the U. S. National Center for Education Statistics (NCES) in their Education Directory** and on the NCES tape of the universe of colleges and universities used to select the sample for this study. The first of these three classes represents the NCES category "Two but less than four years." The second combines two NCES categories "Four or five year baccalaureate" and "Undergraduate non-degree-granting." The third combines the remaining six NCES "highest level of offering" categories, which are: first professional degree, master's, beyond master's but less than doctorate, doctorate, graduate non-degree granting, postdoctoral research only. The NCES directory and tape were used because they show an official list of institutions which "are legally authorized to offer and are offering at least a one-year program of college level studies leading toward a degree."

---

*See Table 12 in Survey of Public Libraries, LIBGIS I (NCES, 1977) and Table 11 in Statistics of Public Libraries, 1977-78 (NCES, 1982).

**For a description of institutions in each category, see pp XIV-XV in Education Directory: Colleges and Universities, 1981-82 (NCES, 1982).

Within each type of library class, libraries were sampled in each of four geographic areas: North Atlantic, Great Lakes and Plains, Southeast, and West and Southwest. A list of states included in each region is provided in Table 25. These regions are used by NCES to stratify the public library universe for the periodic sample surveys conducted by NCES.

Sample selection

Procedures used for the 1984 survey were similar to those used for the 1982 survey. The five type of library classes and four geographic areas were combined to form twenty groups from which samples were selected. As in 1982, we decided that we could afford a survey based on an initial sample of approximately 1400 libraries. Since we expected to get returns from approximately sixty-five percent of those sampled and hoped to get at least twenty-five respondents in each of the twenty groups, the initial mailing should go to at least forty libraries in each group. Once those decisions had been made, we located the smallest of the twenty groups (Large Public Libraries, North Atlantic Region = sixty-one libraries) and calculated the percentage necessary to get a sample return of at least twenty-five libraries. All other groups involving the same type of library (i.e., the three other regions) were sampled with the same percentage. Working within the constraints of the 1400 total and the need for at least twenty-five returns in each group, we sampled all other groups as proportionately as possible. Tables 1-6 (See Chapter 2) show the size of each group, the size of the sample and the size of the return.

Two universe tapes purchased from the National Center for Education Statistics were used to select the sample. For public libraries, we used the 1981 tape of the Public Library Universe. For academic libraries we used the 1982-83 tape of the Institutional Characteristics of Colleges and Universities.

Procedure

For the 1982 survey, an initial draft of the survey questionnaire was prepared by OFR and OLPR. After several revisions, the draft was circulated to all Program Directors on the ALA staff with a request for comments and a pretest of the survey instrument was conducted in November 1981. After the 1982 survey report was published we received several suggestions for change, four of which were made in the 1984 survey. Those changes are explained in the Introduction of this report.

The first mailing of the questionnaire and cover letter was done in early January 1984. A postage paid business reply envelope was enclosed to encourage response. A second mailing was sent to non-respondents in early February. Return rates for each group are shown in Tables 1-6 (See Chapter 2).

The returns were screened at ALA before being sent to the Library Research Center of the University of Illinois School of Library and Information Science (LRC). If necessary, respondents were called to clarify the meaning of information on the return. At the LRC returns were again screened, then edited, and then analyzed by computer using the Statistical Package for the Social Sciences (SPSS).

In addition to the 920 returns which were analyzed, we also received nineteen responses too late for inclusion, fourteen responses which were not useable, and seventy-eight refusals. Two of the fourteen unuseable responses were unclear and we were unable to reach the respondent for clarification; twelve contained salary data but the library was not indentified. Of the seventy-eight refusals, fifteen came from places which could not respond since the institution was closed or reorganized or now served a different population. Fifty-five of the remaining sixty-three gave the following reasons for non-response: no full-time professionals (twenty); all contributed services (thirteen); salary data is confidential (eight); no time available to complete (four); do not have the information (three); major changes are in process (three); do not want to do it (four). Eight returned the questionnaire with identification only and no reason for non-response.

Table 25. States in Four Regions of the U.S.

| North Atlantic | Great Lakes and Plains | Southeast | West and Southwest |
| --- | --- | --- | --- |
| Connecticut | Illinois | Alabama | Alaska |
| Delaware | Indiana | Arkansas | Arizona |
| District of Columbia | Iowa | Florida | California |
| | Kansas | Georgia | Colorado |
| Maine | Michigan | Kentucky | Hawaii |
| Maryland | Minnesota | Louisiana | Idaho |
| Massachusetts | Missouri | Mississippi | Montana |
| New Hampshire | Nebraska | North Carolina | Nevada |
| New Jersey | North Dakota | South Carolina | New Mexico |
| New York | Ohio | Tennessee | Oklahoma |
| Pennsylvania | South Dakota | Virginia | Oregon |
| Rhode Island | Wisconsin | West Virginia | Texas |
| Vermont | | | Utah |
| | | | Washington |
| | | | Wyoming |

Source: <u>Statistics of Public Libraries, 1977-78</u> (NCES, 1982)

Appendix C

## AMERICAN LIBRARY ASSOCIATION

50 EAST HURON STREET · CHICAGO, ILLINOIS 60611 · (312) 944-6780

January 2, 1984

Dear Colleague:

ALA needs your help in providing information to the library community regarding salaries paid for full time professional positions in academic and public libraries of the U. S. Your institution has been selected as part of a sample of libraries which will be asked to complete the enclosed questionnaire. Only summary results will be reported; individual responses will not be identified.

ALA expects the results of this survey to be useful to many people in the library community who need to know what salary might be paid to someone in a particular type of library position or in a particular geographical area. This information is potentially useful to librarians applying for positions, to librarians setting salaries and to many others interested in the compensation of librarians.

ALA collected similar information in 1982 and published the results in a report which sold well and was praised in reviews. We intend to repeat the survey every two years thus establishing a valuable new report series. Because the cooperation of sample libraries is so essential to the success of the survey, participants will receive the report at a special price (to be announced).

Please help your profession by completing the enclosed questionnaire and returning it in the enclosed self-addressed postage paid envelope. If you cannot provide all information requested, please give us as much as possible. The instrument has been designed so that it can be completed in a short amount of time. Please return it as soon as possible but no later than February 10, 1984. If you have questions about the survey please call (collect) Mary Jo Lynch, Director, ALA Office for Research, 312/944-6780. Thank you very much.

Sincerely yours,

Robert Wedgeworth
Robert Wedgeworth
Executive Director

Appendix D

## AMERICAN LIBRARY ASSOCIATION SURVEY OF SALARIES

### Part I. Institutional Data

This section of the questionnaire requests some general information about your library. Neither libraries nor individuals will be identified in the report of this survey. However, we need to know what type of library is responding and where it is located. Also, we may need to contact you if we have questions about your response.

A. Name and address of library: _____

_____

_____

B. Name and title of respondent: _____

C. Telephone number: ( ) _____

D. Type of library responding                                           Circle one

   Public library serving population of from 25,000 to 99,999        1

   Public library serving population of over 100,000                 2

   Library in a 2 year college (offers at least two but less than four years)                                                               3

   Library in a 4 year college (offers four or five year baccalaurelate or four years undergraduate work but not conferring bachelor's degree)   4

   Library in college or university offering work beyond bachelor's level  5

E. Total employee benefits as a percent of total payroll. [Add up the total of what you pay in a year for all benefits you provide to **ALL** library employees (professional, support, others) and divide this total by the amount of your total yearly payroll.]

                                                                                                                                 _____%

F. Within the last 12 months has the library hired any full time professional(s) with a master's degree in library science but no professional experience?

                                                                                                                   Circle one

       No (if so, skip to Section II)                                    1
       Yes                                                                2

G. What is the annual salary paid such a professional(s)? If the library hired more than one, please list all annual salaries below as of January 1, 1984.

| Incumbent | Annual Salary | Incumbent | Annual Salary | Incumbent | Annual Salary |
|---|---|---|---|---|---|
| 1 | _____ | 4 | _____ | 7 | _____ |
| 2 | _____ | 5 | _____ | 8 | _____ |
| 3 | _____ | 6 | _____ | 9 | _____ |

Part II  Professional Position Data

This section of the questionnaire requests information on annual salaries for <u>selected</u> library positions. It does NOT include all positions and we expect that many libraries will have some positions which are not included in the questionnaire.

Each page in Part II contains descriptions of one or more specific library positions. If your library has one or more staff employed full-time whose major responsibilities are covered by the position description, please provide the information requested on the form. If a staff member works full time but performs duties of more than one position, list him or her as incumbent in the position which is his or her major responsibility or in the position having the higher salary. List each staff member only once. All incumbents in these positions should be included regardless of academic credentials and regardless of the number of months worked in a year.* <u>If the incumbent works LESS than a 12 month year</u> (including vacation) please report the salary and circle the appropriate number of months ( 9 or 10) for which the salary is paid.

For each position in which you have staff employed please provide:

A. The starting and maximum annual salary as described in your formal salary schedule. (If you do not have a salary schedule mark "Not Available" in the space provided). This range may cover several levels of positions. Include range for budgeted positions even if position is not currently filled.

B. The annual salary of each incumbent as of January 1, 1984. Give actual dollars paid. Do not include fringe benefits. If you need additional space please use separate sheets of paper. Be sure to indicate the POSITION TITLE as appropriate.


POSITION TITLE:  <u>Director</u>

POSITION DESCRIPTION: Chief administrative officer of the library or library system. Plans and directs all aspects of the operation. May have job title such as Librarian or Head Librarian.

POSITION TITLE: (if different from above)_____

ANNUAL SALARY RANGE:  (from your formal salary schedule)

|  | | |
|---|---|---|
| Starting_____ | 9<br>10 | Note: Circle 9 or 10 ONLY if salary is for LESS than a 12 month year (including vacation). |
| Maximum_____ | 9<br>10 | |
| ANNUAL SALARY  _____ | 9<br>10 | |

*If services are contributed ( i.e. institution pays some expenses or an honorarium but not a true salary) please do not list the incumbent.

POSITION TITLE: <u>Deputy/Associate Director</u>

POSITION DESCRIPTION: Aids Director in planning and directing some or all aspects of library or library system. Is at second-in-command level and may act as Director in the absence of the Director. May manage a major aspect of the library operation (e.g. technical services, public services).

POSITION TITLE: (if different from above)_____

ANNUAL SALARY RANGE: (from your formal salary schedule)

    Starting_____ 9/10

    Maximum_____ 9/10

COMPENSATION DATA:

| Incumbent | Annual Salary |
|---|---|
| 1 | _____ 9/10 |
| 2 | _____ 9/10 |
| 3 | _____ 9/10 |
| 4 | _____ 9/10 |

---

POSITION TITLE: <u>Assistant Director</u> (Note: Incumbents with the title Assistant Director who are second in command and act as Director in the absence of the Director should be listed as Deputy/Associate Director).

POSITION DESCRIPTION: Manages one of the major aspects of the library operation.

POSITION TITLE: (if different from above)_____

ANNUAL SALARY RANGE: (from your formal salary schedule)

    Starting_____ 9/10

    Maximum_____ 9/10

COMPENSATION DATA:

| Incumbent | Annual Salary | Incumbent | Annual Salary | Incumbent | Annual Salary |
|---|---|---|---|---|---|
| 1 | _____ 9/10 | 4 | _____ 9/10 | 7 | _____ 9/10 |
| 2 | _____ 9/10 | 5 | _____ 9/10 | 8 | _____ 9/10 |
| 3 | _____ 9/10 | 6 | _____ 9/10 | 9 | _____ 9/10 |

POSITION TITLE:  Department Head/Branch Head

POSITION DESCRIPTION: Manages operation of a library unit which is physically separate from the main library (e.g. a branch or a department library) or of one aspect of the operation of the main library (e.g. Reference Department, Serials Department, Children's Department).

POSITION TITLE: (if different from above)_____

ANNUAL SALARY RANGE: (from your formal salary schedule)

    Starting_____9/10

    Maximum_____9/10

COMPENSATION DATA:

| Incumbent | Annual Salary | Incumbent | Annual Salary | Incumbent | Annual Salary |
|---|---|---|---|---|---|
| 1 | 9/10 | 5 | 9/10 | 9 | 9/10 |
| 2 | 9/10 | 6 | 9/10 | 10 | 9/10 |
| 3 | 9/10 | 7 | 9/10 | 11 | 9/10 |
| 4 | 9/10 | 8 | 9/10 | 12 | 9/10 |

---

POSITION TITLE:  Reference/Information Librarian

POSITION DESCRIPTION: Locates information for library users or helps users find it. Answers questions and gives instruction about the use of the library. May select materials for the reference collection or general collections. May conduct online searches.

POSITION TITLE: (if different from above)_____

ANNUAL SALARY RANGE: (from your formal salary schedule)

    Starting_____9/10

    Maximum_____9/10

COMPENSATION DATA:

| Incumbent | Annual Salary | Incumbent | Annual Salary | Incumbent | Annual Salary |
|---|---|---|---|---|---|
| 1 | 9/10 | 5 | 9/10 | 9 | 9/10 |
| 2 | 9/10 | 6 | 9/10 | 10 | 9/10 |
| 3 | 9/10 | 7 | 9/10 | 11 | 9/10 |
| 4 | 9/10 | 8 | 9/10 | 12 | 9/10 |

POSITION TITLE: <u>Cataloger and/or Classifier</u>

POSITION DESCRIPTION: Organizes materials purchased and received by the library. Describes each item in standard format and assigns access points. Assigns subject headings and classification numbers to library materials. May supervise assistants who prepare catalog cards. May be involved with only descriptive cataloging or only subject cataloging/classification.

POSITION TITLE: (if different from above)_____

ANNUAL SALARY RANGE: (from your formal salary schedule)

Starting _____ 9/10

Maximum _____ 9/10

COMPENSATION DATA:

| Incumbent | Annual Salary | Incumbent | Annual Salary | Incumbent | Annual Salary |
|---|---|---|---|---|---|
| 1 | ____ 9/10 | 5 | ____ 9/10 | 9 | ____ 9/10 |
| 2 | ____ 9/10 | 6 | ____ 9/10 | 10 | ____ 9/10 |
| 3 | ____ 9/10 | 7 | ____ 9/10 | 11 | ____ 9/10 |
| 4 | ____ 9/10 | 8 | ____ 9/10 | 12 | ____ 9/10 |

POSITION TITLE: <u>Serials Librarian</u>

POSITION DESCRIPTION: Facilitates selection, acquisition, organization and use of the library's serial publications.

POSITION TITLE: (if different from above)_____

ANNUAL SALARY RANGE: (from your formal salary schedule)

Starting _____ 9/10

Maximum _____ 9/10

COMPENSATION DATA:

| Incumbent | Annual Salary | Incumbent | Annual Salary | Incumbent | Annual Salary |
|---|---|---|---|---|---|
| 1 | ____ 9/10 | 5 | ____ 9/10 | 9 | ____ 9/10 |
| 2 | ____ 9/10 | 6 | ____ 9/10 | 10 | ____ 9/10 |
| 3 | ____ 9/10 | 7 | ____ 9/10 | 11 | ____ 9/10 |
| 4 | ____ 9/10 | 8 | ____ 9/10 | 12 | ____ 9/10 |

POSITION TITLE: <u>Audiovisual Librarian</u>

POSITION DESCRIPTION: Facilitates acquisition, organization and use of the library's collection of audiovisual material. May plan and conduct audiovisual programs and services. May supervise production of materials (e.g. video programs).

POSITION TITLE: (if different from above)_____

ANNUAL SALARY RANGE: (from your formal salary schedule)

Starting _____ 9/10

Maximum _____ 9/10

COMPENSATION DATA:

| Incumbent | Annual Salary | Incumbent | Annual Salary | Incumbent | Annual Salary |
|---|---|---|---|---|---|
| 1 | _____ 9/10 | 5 | _____ 9/10 | 9 | _____ 9/10 |
| 2 | _____ 9/10 | 6 | _____ 9/10 | 10 | _____ 9/10 |
| 3 | _____ 9/10 | 7 | _____ 9/10 | 11 | _____ 9/10 |
| 4 | _____ 9/10 | 8 | _____ 9/10 | 12 | _____ 9/10 |

---

POSITION TITLE: <u>Government Documents Librarian</u>

POSITION DESCRIPTION: Facilitates selection, acquisition, organization and use of the government document materials collection.

POSITION TITLE (if different from above)_____

ANNUAL SALARY RANGE: (from your formal salary schedule)

Starting _____ 9/10

Maximum _____ 9/10

COMPENSATION DATA:

| Incumbent | Annual Salary | Incumbent | Annual Salary | Incumbent | Annual Salary |
|---|---|---|---|---|---|
| 1 | _____ 9/10 | 5 | _____ 9/10 | 9 | _____ 9/10 |
| 2 | _____ 9/10 | 6 | _____ 9/10 | 10 | _____ 9/10 |
| 3 | _____ 9/10 | 7 | _____ 9/10 | 11 | _____ 9/10 |
| 4 | _____ 9/10 | 8 | _____ 9/10 | 12 | _____ 9/10 |

POSITION TITLE: <u>Subject Specialist/Bibliographer</u>

POSITION DESCRIPTION: Selects materials in one or more specialized subject areas. May also facilitate acquisition, organization and use of library collections in a specific subject area. May provide specialized reference service, compile bibliographies of library materials in a subject area or provide other specialized services.

POSITION TITLE: (if different from above)_____

ANNUAL SALARY RANGE: (from your formal salary schedule)

Starting _____ 9/10

Maximum _____ 9/10

COMPENSATION DATA:

| Incumbent | Annual Salary | Incumbent | Annual Salary | Incumbent | Annual Salary |
|---|---|---|---|---|---|
| 1 | _____ 9/10 | 5 | _____ 9/10 | 9 | _____ 9/10 |
| 2 | _____ 9/10 | 6 | _____ 9/10 | 10 | _____ 9/10 |
| 3 | _____ 9/10 | 7 | _____ 9/10 | 11 | _____ 9/10 |
| 4 | _____ 9/10 | 8 | _____ 9/10 | 12 | _____ 9/10 |

POSITION TITLE: <u>Children's and/or Young Adult Services Librarian</u>

POSITION DESCRIPTION: Plans and conducts library services for children and/or young adults. Advises on reading materials. May select materials for the collection. May plan and conduct special programs and outreach services.

POSITION TITLE: (if different from above)_____

ANNUAL SALARY RANGE: (from your formal salary schedule)

Starting_____

Maximum_____

COMPENSATION DATA:

| Incumbent | Annual Salary | Incumbent | Annual Salary | Incumbent | Annual Salary |
|---|---|---|---|---|---|
| 1 | _____ | 5 | _____ | 9 | _____ |
| 2 | _____ | 6 | _____ | 10 | _____ |
| 3 | _____ | 7 | _____ | 11 | _____ |
| 4 | _____ | 8 | _____ | 12 | _____ |

(please turn over)

POSITION TITLE:   Adult Services Librarian

POSITION DESCRIPTION:  Plans and conducts library services for adults. Advises on reading materials.  May select materials for the collection.  May plan and conduct special programs and outreach services.

POSITION TITLE:   (if different from above)_____

ANNUAL SALARY RANGE:   (from your formal salary schedule)

    Starting_____

    Maximum_____

COMPENSATION DATA:

| Incumbent | Annual Salary | Incumbent | Annual Salary | Incumbent | Annual Salary |
|---|---|---|---|---|---|
| 1 | _____ | 5 | _____ | 9 | _____ |
| 2 | _____ | 6 | _____ | 10 | _____ |

---

POSITION TITLE:   Coordinator, Adult and/or Young Adult and/or Children's Services

POSITION DESCRIPTION:  Coordinates all services to adults and/or young adults and/or children in the library system.  Manages selection of materials. Maintains relationships with community groups.

POSITION TITLE:   (if different from above)_____

ANNUAL SALARY RANGE:   (from your formal salary schedule)

    Starting_____

    Maximum_____

COMPENSATION DATA:

| Incumbent | Annual Salary |
|---|---|
| 1 | _____ |
| 2 | _____ |
| 3 | _____ |
| 4 | _____ |

Thank you very much!  Please return by February 10th in enclosed postage paid envelope to:

    American Library Association
    Office for Research
    50 E. Huron
    Chicago, Illinois 60611

APPENDIX E

SALARIES PAID FOR LESS THAN A TWELVE MONTH YEAR IN ACADEMIC LIBRARIES

Instructions on page two of the questionnaire told the respondent:

If the incumbent works LESS than a 12 month year (including vacation) please report the salary and circle the appropriate number of months (9 or 10) for which the salary is paid.

A program was written to prorate these salaries to their twelve month equivalents for the purpose of reporting results of this survey. For each position in which nine or ten month salaries paid were reported, Table 26 gives the total number of incumbents, the number and percent of nine month salaries, the number and percent of ten month salaries and the total number and percent of nine and ten month salaries.

Table 26. Salaries Paid for Less than a 12 Month Year in Academic Libraries by Position and Type of Library.

| Position and Type of Library | All Incumbents # | 9-month # | 9-month % | 10-month # | 10-month % | 9 & 10 month # | 9 & 10 month % |
|---|---|---|---|---|---|---|---|
| **Director** | | | | | | | |
| 2-year college | 150 | 15 | 10 | 11 | 7 | 26 | 17 |
| 4-year college | 100 | 3 | 3 | 12 | 12 | 15 | 15 |
| University | 155 | 3 | 2 | 3 | 2 | 6 | 4 |
| **Associate Director** | | | | | | | |
| 2-year college | 31 | 7 | 23 | 1 | 3 | 8 | 26 |
| 4-year college | 25 | 1 | 4 | 1 | 4 | 2 | 8 |
| University | 101 | 3 | 3 | 3 | 3 | 6 | 6 |
| **Assistant Director** | | | | | | | |
| 2-year college | 24 | 3 | 13 | 1 | 4 | 4 | 17 |
| 4-year college | 15 | 1 | 7 | 0 | 0 | 1 | 7 |
| University | 104 | 3 | 3 | 10 | 10 | 13 | 13 |
| **Department Head** | | | | | | | |
| 2-year college | 24 | 6 | 25 | 3 | 13 | 9 | 38 |
| 4-year college | 30 | 3 | 10 | 4 | 13 | 7 | 23 |
| University | 491 | 15 | 3 | 24 | 5 | 39 | 8 |

(continued next page)

Table 26. (cont.) Salaries Paid for Less than a 12 Month Year in Academic Libraries by Position and Type of Library.

| Position and Type of Library | All Incumbents # | 9-month # | 9-month % | 10-month # | 10-month % | 9 & 10 month # | 9 & 10 month % |
|---|---|---|---|---|---|---|---|
| **Reference/Information Librarian** | | | | | | | |
| 2-year college | 105 | 21 | 20 | 40 | 38 | 61 | 58 |
| 4-year college | 59 | 7 | 12 | 10 | 17 | 17 | 29 |
| University | 488 | 23 | 5 | 42 | 9 | 65 | 13 |
| **Cataloger and/or Classifier** | | | | | | | |
| 2-year college | 44 | 7 | 16 | 13 | 30 | 20 | 45 |
| 4-year college | 59 | 4 | 7 | 8 | 14 | 12 | 20 |
| University | 350 | 10 | 3 | 21 | 6 | 31 | 9 |
| **Serials Librarian** | | | | | | | |
| 2-year college | 12 | 1 | 8 | 5 | 42 | 6 | 50 |
| 4-year college | 19 | 3 | 16 | 3 | 16 | 6 | 32 |
| University | 89 | 4 | 4 | 3 | 3 | 7 | 8 |
| **Audiovisual Librarian** | | | | | | | |
| 2-year college | 38 | 6 | 16 | 5 | 13 | 11 | 29 |
| 4-year college | 28 | 3 | 11 | 2 | 7 | 5 | 18 |
| University | 49 | 2 | 4 | 3 | 6 | 5 | 10 |
| **Government Documents Librarian** | | | | | | | |
| 2-year college | 0 | 0 | 0 | 0 | 0 | 0 | 0 |
| 4-year college | 4 | 0 | 0 | 1 | 25 | 1 | 25 |
| University | 74 | 3 | 4 | 4 | 5 | 7 | 9 |
| **Subject Specialist/ Bibliographer** | | | | | | | |
| 2-year college | 4 | 0 | 0 | 3 | 75 | 3 | 75 |
| 4-year college | 8 | 2 | 25 | 0 | 0 | 2 | 25 |
| University | 146 | 5 | 3 | 13 | 9 | 18 | 12 |

Source: ALA SURVEY OF LIBRARIAN SALARIES, 1984.

Z
682.3
L92
1984

AUG 3 0 1984

RAYMOND H. FOGLER LIBRARY
**DATE DUE**

BOOKS ARE SUBJECT TO
RECALL AFTER TWO WEEKS